DISCOVER THE PULSE POTENTIAL

PEAS BEANS LENTILS CHICKPEAS

INCLUDES NUTRITIONAL ANALYSIS & DIABETIC FOOD CHOICES

BY
THE SASKATCHEWAN PULSE CROP DEVELOPMENT BOARD

FRONT COVER
COUSCOUS WITH AUTUMN VEGETABLES, page 100

DISCOVER THE PULSE POTENTIAL

by
The Saskatchewan Pulse Crop Development Board

First Printing, August 1994

Canadian Cataloguing in Publication Data
Discover the pulse potential
   Includes index,
   ISBN 1-895292-45-X
1. Cookery (Legumes)   2. Gluten-free diet — Recipes.
I. Saskatchewan Pulse Crop Development Board.

TX 803.P4D5 1994   641.6'565   C94-920210-X

Photography: Jerry Humeny, Black Box Images, Saskatoon, Saskatchewan
Tableware: Courtesy of Bon Vivant, The Art of Good Living,
         115 Bayside Centre, Saskatoon, Saskatchewan

Food Styling: LeeAnn Bodnaryk
         Linda Braun, Food Focus Saskatoon, Inc.

Recipe Development and Testing: Food Focus Saskatoon, Inc.

Nutrient Analysis and Diabetic Food Choices:
Joanne Smart, B.S., PDt. and Shirlinie Varde, M.Sc.
College of Pharmacy and Nutrition, University of Saskatchewan

Gluten-Free Identification: Myrna Laycock, P.Dt. Clinical Dietitian
         Royal University Hospital
         Joslyn Fritz, P.Dt.
         Shelley Case, P.Dt. Outpatient Dietitian
         Regina Health District

Designed, Printed and Produced in Canada by
Centax Books, a division of PrintWest Communications Ltd.
Publishing Director: Margo Embury
1150 Eighth Avenue, Regina, Saskatchewan, Canada S4R 1C9
(306) 525-2304   FAX (306) 757-2439

Table of Contents

Gluten-free recipes have been identified. However, please check product labels to make sure ingredients are in fact gluten-free.

Recipes have been tested in both metric and U.S. standard measurements.

Pulse Crop Development Board

P.O. Box 516, Regina, Canada S4P 3A2

The Saskatchewan Pulse Crop Development Board is proud to present a new and exciting cookbook — *Discover the Pulse Potential*. Responding to international market demands for high-quality peas, beans, lentils and chickpeas, Saskatchewan farmers have used their natural advantage of near-ideal soils and growing conditions, together with their expertise in dryland farming to put the best pulses in the world on the market.

As some of these pulses were new to many North Americans, the growers published a cookbook *The Amazing Legume* in the 1980s to show how to cook delicious, nutritious and economical meals. *The Amazing Legume* has gone into its seventh printing, indicating tremendous interest in these old but new foods.

Consumers of the 90s are placing more and more emphasis on nutrition and this new cookbook has been created to provide all the nutritional information needed on pulses, as well as tips on identifying, buying and storing peas, beans, lentils and chickpeas.

This cookbook also recognizes that people no longer have time to stir and simmer their food for hours and there are many fast and tasty recipes included.

We are proud of the pulses that we grow and with the help of this cookbook, you, the consumer, will be proud of the meals you prepare with them.

Sincerely,
Saskatchewan Pulse Crop Development Board

Keith Cheston, Chair
Domestic Market Development Committee

The Saskatchewan Canola Development Commission is pleased to endorse this new and inspiring cookbook, ***Discover the Pulse Potential***. Saskatchewan farmers are proud of the food products they produce. With increasing trade globalization, Saskatchewan's nutritious food products, such as pulses and canola oil, are finding their place, not only on Canadian tables, but on food tables around the world. This is just another example of Saskatchewan farmers keeping pace with changing food habits.

Upon reading this cookbook, you will be impressed, not only with the variety of recipes, but also with the handy reference guide for buying, storing and using pulses.

The recipes in this cookbook call for canola oil and canola oil products. Canola oil is low in saturated fats and high in monounsaturated and polyunsaturated fatty acids. Like all vegetable oils, canola oil is cholesterol-free. So, discover for yourself the pulse and canola potential in this cookbook.

Sincerely,
Saskatchewan Canola Development Commission

John Christensen
General Manager

CANADIAN CELIAC
ASSOCIATION

L'ASSOCIATION
CANADIENNE
DE LA MALADIE
COELIAQUE

6519B Mississauga Road, Mississauga, Ontario L5N 1A6 (905) 567-7195 Fax: (905) 567-0710

As Celiacs and supporters of Celiacs, we are always looking to broaden our horizons. Our food focus (free of gluten), as the treatment for Celiac Disease, presents an ongoing dilemma of "What To Cook?" that the whole family can eat.

The vast potential of pulses presents a very real solution for every age group, background and economic situation, and most importantly for those of us with gluten intolerance. Gluten is a protein present in wheat, rye, triticale, barley and oats. It is toxic to those with Celiac Disease. The only treatment is a diet free of gluten.

With an array of nutritional and flavorful recipes, which are also eye- and taste-appealing, the Saskatchewan Pulse Crop Development Board has come along with a winner!

From main courses to desserts, some recipes are naturally gluten-free, but remember when using package ingredients, that label-reading is an art and must be continually "fine-tuned." Contact the Canadian Celiac Association for books, videos, resource material and counseling information. Call 1-800-363-7296.

Sincerely,
Canadian Celiac Association

Gwen Shaver
President

The Canadian Cancer Society recommends a diet based on Canada's Guidelines for Healthy Eating. These are:

1. Enjoy a VARIETY of foods.

2. Emphasize cereals, breads, other grain products, vegetables and fruits.

3. Choose lower-fat dairy products, leaner meats and foods prepared with little or no fat.

4. Achieve and maintain a healthy body weight by enjoying regular physical activity and healthy eating.

5   Limit salt, alcohol and caffeine.

Pulses are an important part of a healthy diet and are included in Canada's Food Guide to Healthy Eating. They are a good source of fiber and other nutrients. They are also low in cost, and can be prepared in a variety of appetizing ways.

Your new cookbook contains recipes which will enable Canadians to experiment with different, tasty and health-promoting meals.

Yours in health,

Nutrition Expert Advisory Group
Canadian Cancer Society

Pulse Crop Development Board

P.O. Box 516, Regina, Canada S4P 3A2

Dear Reader:

This book has been designed to help you **Discover the Pulse Potential** through nutritional information and delicious recipes for pulse cooking. Use the following tips to help you discover pulses and use this book to its full potential!

- Recipes, when convenient, have been developed using precooked pulses. Cooked peas, beans, lentils and chickpeas can be refrigerated up to three days or frozen up to six months. Precooking pulses and storing them in amounts suitable for your favorite soup, salad, main dish or dessert is a real time-saver. We are also seeing more and more canned, ready-to-serve pulses on the market. These recipes can easily be adapted to use canned pulses.

  A 398 mL (14 oz.) can of drained pulses approximately equals 375 mL (1½ cups) cooked pulses. A 540 mL (19 oz.) can of drained pulses approximately equals 500 mL (2 cups) cooked pulses.

- We have identified gluten-free recipes. We trust that you will use only gluten-free ingredients for these.

- Per serving nutrient breakdown and diabetic food choices accompany each recipe. Dietary fiber calculations are based on the Englyst method. Diabetic food choices are based on the Good Health Eating Guide (1994) from the Canadian Diabetes Association. Complete nutritional analysis is available upon request from the Saskatchewan Pulse Crop Development Board.

- *When purchasing pulses they are often not labeled according to their variety name as in our recipes (i.e. Eston, Laird, Rose ...). See page 17 for a description of each variety.*

- Each recipe indicates which pulse product is used in the recipe. Eston, Gold and Laird lentils have slightly different cooking properties and flavours but can easily be substituted for each other. The same is true for yellow and green peas and all varieties of beans.

- Each recipe has been tested in U.S. standard and metric measures. Cooks should use either metric or U.S. standard in each recipe, not a combination of both.

- Use these recipes as a base and create your own exciting pulse recipes.

We hope you find this an informative, easy to use cookbook! Happy Cooking!

Regards,
Saskatchewan Pulse Crop Development Board

Linda Braun, B.S.H.Ec.
Home Economics Consultant

Dorothy Long, B.S.H.Ec.; B.Ed.
Home Economics Consultant

The Past of Pulses

"Pulse," derived from the Latin puls, a potage or thick soup, is the broad term used to describe dried edible seeds of legumes — specifically peas, beans, lentils and chickpeas.

The history of pulses dates back more than 10,000 years and spans the globe. Graphic records of their use were found in the Egyptian pyramids, while in Switzerland dry peas were discovered in a village dating back to the Stone Age. Lentils, sometimes thinly coated with gold, were one of the favorite dishes of the ancient Greeks. In Britain, peas were grown as early as the 11th century. They were considered a staple in the diet and recognized in this old English nursery rhyme . .

> Pease pudding hot
> Pease pudding cold
> Pease pudding in the pot, nine days old.

Mrs. Beeton, author of the classic Victorian cookbook, *Mrs. Beeton's Cookery,* describes the Pease pudding as an "exceedingly nice accompaniment to boiled beef."

Pulses played a colorful part in the history of North America as well, in the hearty pea soup the early French settlers introduced to Canadians and in the diets of pioneers who helped develop the West. Baked beans were considered a staple for ranchers riding the winter trail. They froze beans, in batches, carved off their daily portion and heated it over an open fire.

Baked beans continue to play a central part in menus for rodeos and barbecues.

The Pulse Potential: Pulses in a Healthy Diet

Healthy eating, now recognized as a way to actively promote health and help reduce the risk of nutrition-related problems such as heart disease, cancer and obesity, is the foundation of Canada's Food Guide to Healthy Eating introduced in 1993.

Dried peas, beans, lentils and chickpeas (pulses) fit the overall healthy eating pattern encouraged by the guide because they are low in fat and good sources of protein, starch and fiber.

Pulses are located in the meat and alternatives group in the Guide because consumers often use them as a substitute for meat. They could easily be included in the grain products group as well because they contain similar nutrients, such as carbohydrates and fiber.

Reducing fat content in the diet is an important part of the Guide's intent and one of the strategies recommended to reduce the risk of heart attack. Choosing leaner meats or using alternatives such as peas, beans, lentils and chickpeas more often is emphasized. The fat content of meat and alternatives varies considerably from foods such as lentils and dried peas, which contain very little fat, to some cold cuts such as salami which are classified as high fat foods.

Complex Carbohydrates

Consumers are encouraged by the Guide to increase their intake of carbohydrates and fiber. Canadian nutrition recommendations advise that the increase in carbohydrates should come from foods rich in complex carbohydrates (starch). It is suggested that the Canadian diet should provide 55 percent of energy as carbohydrates from a variety of sources. "Eating patterns that are high in complex carbohydrates and fiber are associated with a lower incidence of heart disease and certain types of cancer."

Many consumers believe starchy foods are fattening, but staple forms of starchy foods like bread, rice, pasta, potatoes and pulses are very low in fat.

Fiber

The Guide encourages increased consumption of dietary fiber by promoting the use of more whole-grain products, vegetables, fruit, dried peas, beans, lentils and chickpeas. Canadians are being encouraged to increase their intake of fiber to 25 to 30 grams per day. Dried peas, beans, lentils and chickpeas are excellent sources.

Different forms of fiber perform different functions in the body.

Soluble fiber, found in beans, peas, chickpeas, oat bran, fruits and lentils, forms a gel inside the digestive system and is thought to reduce cholesterol levels in the blood and delay entry of sugar into the blood stream. The delayed entry of sugar into the blood stream appears to stabilize blood sugar levels, so pulses are beneficial for diabetics.

Insoluble fiber, found in peas, beans and lentils, wheat bran, vegetables, fruits, whole grains and breads, improves regularity by speeding up the passage of food through the intestine and is believed to have a role in the prevention of colon cancer.

Because of their high starch and fiber content, nutrition researchers suggest pulses may prove to be of considerable benefit in the prevention of colonic disease and other nutrition-related health problems. Peas, beans and lentils contain both types of fiber. Lentils contain mainly insoluble fiber, while peas and beans contain both. Because green lentils are consumed with their seed coat intact they have almost twice the amount of fiber of imported red lentils.

Folic Acid

Pulses are rich in the B-vitamin, folic acid. Many recent research publications indicate a conclusive link between intake and the occurrence of Neural Tube Defects in infants. A low intake of folic acid by the mother just before and after conception puts the fetus at risk of birth defects such as spina bifida, anencephaly and encephalocoele which are caused by malformations of the embryonic neural tube.

The risk factor is increased if a woman has previously given birth to a NTD infant. Other factors include poor nutrition and use of drugs that interfere with folic acid metabolism, such anticonvulsants, alcohol and birth control pills.

The current Canadian Recommended Nutrient Intake (RNI) for folic acid is approximately 180 micrograms (µg) for a woman. During pregnancy the RNI is more than doubled, to almost 400 µg (0.4 mg) per day. Research suggests this should be raised for women throughout their child-bearing years to 400 µg (0.4 mg) per day to ensure stores of folic acid in the body are sufficient at conception and during early fetal development. This level prevents complications from arising before the woman knows she is pregnant. As a defect in folic acid

Excellent Sources of Folic Acid
(Based on 250 mL [1 cup])

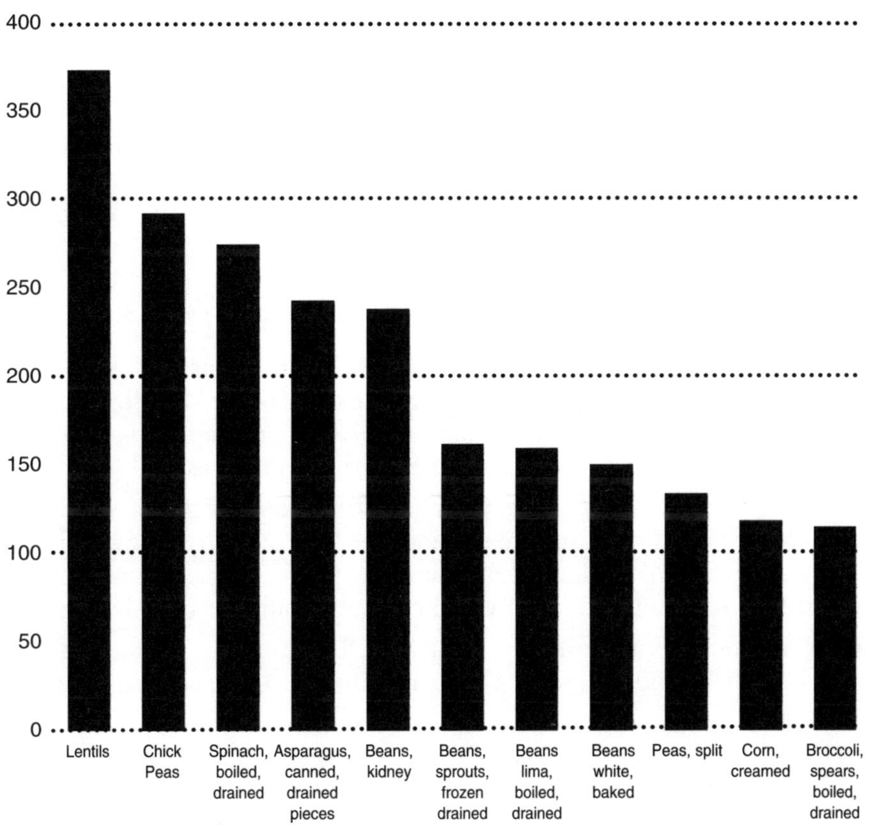

(Source: Health and Welfare Canada (1988), *Nutrient Value of Some Common Foods*)

metabolism is more likely in high-risk women who have had a previous NTD child, it is most important to increase their intake to 4000 µg (4 mg) per day prior to conception.

11

By eating a variety of foods, including leafy greens, citrus fruits, yeast, dried peas, beans, lentils and chickpeas, or fortified breakfast cereals, women can ingest significant folic acid while maintaining an overall balanced diet. Even small servings (less than 125 mL [½ cup]) of lentils and other pulses provide excellent sources of folic acid.

Potassium

Pulses are an excellent source of potassium, which contributes to a regular heart beat, regulates transfer of nutrients to cells, controls water balance and helps regulate blood pressure.

B Vitamins

Pulses are good sources of niacin, thiamin, pantothenic acid and pyridoxine, necessary for healthy brain and nerve cells, for normal functioning of the skin nerves and digestive system and in the chemical reactions of amino acids and proteins.

Protein

Pulses are good sources of vegetable protein, which must be combined with a complementary protein to become a complete protein containing the nine essential amino acids. Pulses, when eaten with nuts, seeds, rice or grains, fulfill the requirements of a complete protein.

The Pulse Potential: Pulses in the Special Diet

Diabetes is a condition affecting the body's ability to control blood sugar levels, which rise during the digestion of food. Insulin is the stabilizing hormone controlling the absorption of blood sugar. If insulin production is faulty, blood sugar levels can rise dangerously high, resulting in diabetes.

Researchers have shown consumption of fiber along with carbohydrates appears to lower insulin requirements and keeps blood sugar levels in check, so pulses are beneficial to diabetics. The dietary fiber in pulses seems to slow the digestive process and the absorption of sugars into the blood stream.

Food Choice Values assigned to the recipes in this book are in accordance with the Good Health Eating Guide (1994) and will help those with diabetes make educated choices.

Celiac Disease is a gastrointestinal disorder in which the absorptive surface of the small intestine is damaged by gluten — a protein found in wheat, rye, triticale, barley and oats. As a result, the body cannot absorb protein, fat, carbohydrates, vitamins and minerals. The only treatment is a life-long, gluten-free diet. Symptoms of celiac disease vary widely and may include weight loss, chronic diarrhea, bulky stools, cramps and bloating, malnutrition, flatulence, fatigue, irritability and anemia. A biopsy of the small intestine must be performed to confirm celiac disease. A trial gluten-free diet is not recommended.

Pulses are an important component in the gluten-free diet. They add variety to a diet which must be followed for life and are a good source of the B vitamins thiamin and niacin, nutrients often lacking in a gluten-free diet. They are also a source of calcium necessary for healthy bones. This is important for individuals with celiac disease because many also cannot digest lactose, the sugar found in milk, which means they need sources of calcium other than milk. Pulses are an excellent source of potassium, which recent studies suggest may decrease calcium loss in the urine.

Fiber can be difficult to acquire in a gluten-free diet because of the restriction on grains. As pulses are high in fiber they help prevent constipation.

Gluten-free recipes are identified. Gluten is a binder used in many processed products; as a precaution read the label or check with the manufacturer to ensure you are using gluten-free products. The following is a partial list of products to check before using: mayonnaise, beef or chicken soup base, vegetable soup mix, bouillon cubes, sausage, salad dressings, soy sauce, icing sugar, Mexican spiced tomatoes, curry powder, peanut butter, paprika, canned soups, Worcestershire sauce, mixed spices and seasonings.

Osteoporosis is characterized by a decrease in bone mass and increased susceptibility to fractures. Both men and women lose bone mass as they age, but the process accelerates for women with the onset of menopause.

Regular physical activity and a well-balanced diet, including enough calcium each day, are important to keep bones healthy. Consuming less calcium than your body requires over a long period of time means the body will take calcium from the bones, leaving the bones porous, brittle and breakable. Dietary calcium intake throughout life is important. Dairy products, particularly milk, yogurt and cheese, are important sources.

A number of other nutrients help in building bone and the absorption of calcium including vitamin D, manganese, fluoride, potassium and protein.

Protein is available from a number of food sources including meat, pulses, grains, vegetables and dairy products. In fact, people consuming mainly plant-based foods may have a lower requirement for calcium. Pulses are a good source of plant-based protein. Just one serving, 250 mL (1 cup), of pulses provides approximately16 grams of protein, almost one-third of the recommended daily intake.

Pulses are an excellent source of potassium. Recent studies suggest potassium may decrease the amount of calcium lost in the urine which could mean less bone loss. A study performed at the University of Saskatchewan in 1992 showed subjects lost an average 35 percent less calcium in the urine when consuming a diet with added potassium bicarbonate, an alkaline potassium source which simulates a high vegetable diet.

Some studies have suggested that phytate, a substance found in food containing dietary fiber, such as pulses, may decrease the absorption of dietary calcium from the intestine. But a University of Saskatchewan study showed that adding 125 mL (½ cup) of lentils to the daily diets of adult males had no negative effect on calcium absorption.

Vegetarianism

Changing eating trends indicate that more people have vegetarian or semi-vegetarian diets. Studies show that vegetarians are closer to their optimal weight and tend to be less at risk for heart disease, colon cancer, diabetes, high blood pressure and high cholesterol levels.

Choosing a vegetarian diet requires planning to include essential nutrients. With careful planning vegetarians are no more prone to nutritional deficiencies than meat-eaters.

Pulses are excellent sources of vegetable protein and iron.

There are two kinds of iron: organic or heme iron (found in meat, easily absorbed by the body) and inorganic or nonheme iron (found in plant-related foods, not as easily absorbed). Iron absorption, heme or nonheme, from any source varies according to the source of the iron, the presence of other substances and the health of the individual.

To retain the maximum value of iron from pulses or other foods, they should be eaten in meals that include a variety of food to enhance the iron absorption. Vitamin C is especially good at enhancing iron use by our bodies. Cast iron cooking pots also contribute iron.

Protein is made up of amino acids which are necessary for the maintenance of the human body. There are two types of protein — complete protein, which contains all the essential amino acids, and incomplete protein, which contains only some of the essential amino acids. Essential amino acids are the nine amino acids the body cannot produce and therefore they must come from food sources.

Protein from animal sources, such as eggs, milk, cheese and meats, is complete protein while protein from plant sources, such as pulses, nuts and cereals, is incomplete protein. Incomplete protein is used more effectively by the body when combined with a complementary incomplete protein or a complete protein, such as meat, than if eaten separately.

Complementary protein is formed by combining two or more proteins which provide all the essential amino acids needed daily. For example, protein found in lentils is low in methionine and high in lysine. When combined with a complementary protein, such as grains or nuts, which is high in methionine and low in lysine, all essential amino acids are present in sufficient amounts and each incomplete protein is used more efficiently by the body.

Types of vegetarian diets include:

Vegans:	strict vegetarians who abstain from eating all foods of animal origin.
Lactovegetarians:	include dairy products in their diet but abstain from other animal-origin foods.
Lacto-ovovegetarians:	include eggs and dairy products but exclude other animal-origin foods.
Semivegetarians:	include eggs, dairy and occasionally meat products in their diet.

Complementary Protein Chart

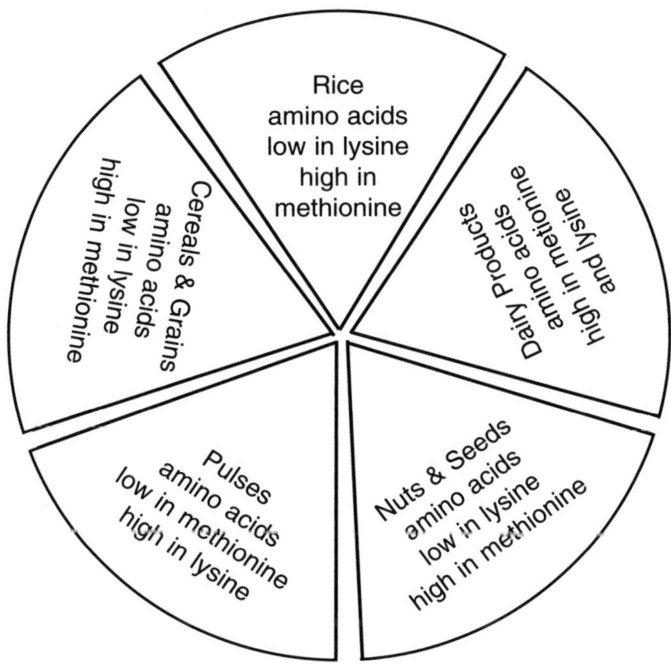

By following the chart, pulses can be combined with another food that is high in their missing amino acids, for example:

    pulses + cereals/grains

    pulses + nuts/seeds

    pulses + rice

    pulses + dairy products

Each of these combinations makes a complete protein that fulfills human requirements. Complementary foods do not have to be consumed at the same meal to achieve a complete protein. Just make sure the complementary proteins are eaten within a few hours of each other.

Pulse Preparation

Buying

Pulses come in numerous shapes, sizes and colors. Generally, when buying dried pulse products, look for bright color, uniform size and smooth skins without chips or shrivelled seed coats. Dry product sometimes contains foreign material, such as small pebbles and bits of soil; therefore, always sort and rinse pulses before cooking.

Lentils, peas, beans and chickpeas can be found in most supermarkets, health food stores and ethnic food specialty stores. They are available in bulk, packaged in plastic bags or canned. Canned pulses can conveniently be drained, rinsed and added to recipes calling for precooked product.

Note: A 540 mL (19 oz.) can of drained pulses is approximately equivalent to 500 mL (2 cups) of cooked pulses. A 398 mL (14 oz.) can of drained pulses is approximately equivalent to 375 mL (1½ cups) of cooked pulses.

Storing

Dry lentils, peas, beans and chickpeas will keep almost indefinitely if stored in tightly covered containers in a dry place at below 21°C (70°F). When exposed to light, pulses tend to lose their color, but flavor, nutrition and texture will not be affected as long as they are tightly sealed. However, the longer a pulse is stored, the drier it becomes. This results in a product that takes longer to cook and may remain slightly chewy after cooking. It is best to use dry pulses within one year of purchase.

Save on meal preparation time by cooking more beans, peas or lentils than needed for one meal and store in the refrigerator or freezer. To refrigerate: cool the cooked pulses then store in the cooking water. If there is insufficient cooking water to cover the pulses, add boiled water to prevent the pulses from drying out. Store in a covered container for one to three days. To freeze: cool the pulses, then store in plastic, metal or glass containers or plastic bags. Fill the container ⅔ full. Freeze in 250 to 500 mL (1 to 2 cup) portions, ready to add to soups, casseroles or other favorite dishes.

Soaking Methods

Before soaking or cooking dry pulses, "pick them over" to remove dried soil, small pebbles and other foreign material. Then rinse and drain.

The Long Soak or Overnight Method:
For every 250 mL (1 cup) of beans or whole peas, add 750 mL (3 cups) of water. Let stand 12 hours or overnight. Discard soaking water and cook beans or peas according to recipe.

The Quick Soak Method:
For every 250 mL (1 cup) of beans or whole peas, add 750 mL (3 cups) of water. Slowly bring to a boil and boil gently for 2 minutes. Remove from heat, cover and let stand 1 hour. Discard soaking water and cook according to recipe. Using this method, beans absorb as much water in 1 hour as they do in 15 hours soaking in cold water.

Microwave Soak Method:
Combine beans or whole peas and water in a 4 L (4-quart) microwave-safe casserole. Cover. Microwave on full power (High) 15 minutes, or until boiling. Let stand 1 hour. Drain.

Peas

Field peas are usually round seeds with a translucent seed coat. Field peas are grown in Manitoba, Alberta and Saskatchewan. Dry yellow peas, whole or split, are the main type grown, with green peas making up a small percentage of production. Whole peas require soaking before cooking while splits do not.

Peas	Description	Soaking Method	Cooking Time
Yellow	• yellow cotyledon • available whole or split • excellent in soups and salads • used as bird seed in some countries	Whole: quick or long Split: no soak	Whole: 1½ to 2 hours Split: 40 to 45 minutes For Purée: Cook 45 to 60 minutes
Green	• green cotyledon • available whole or split • traditionally used for pea soup (French Canadian)	Whole: quick or long Split: no soak	Whole: 1½ to 2 hours Split: 40 to 45 minutes For Purée: Cook 45 to 60 minutes

Lentils

Lentils are circular, flat, lens-shaped seeds usually found with a green seed coat. They are grown mainly in Saskatchewan, Alberta and Manitoba. They require no presoaking, cook rapidly and can be used as vegetables in soups, salads and casseroles or puréed and added to baked products. Lentils make excellent sprouts.

Lentils	Description	Soaking Method	Cooking Time
Laird	• 6 mm across • light green seed coat and yellow cotyledon • nutty flavor • great in soups and purées	No soak	30 to 40 minutes cook 45 to 50 minutes for purée
Eston	• 4 to 4.5 mm across • light green seed coat and yellow cotyledon • nutty flavor • retain their shape after cooking • well suited to salads and soups	No soak	30 to 40 minutes For purée: cook 45 to 50 minutes
Rose (Split)	• light green seed coat and red cotyledon • sold commercially with the seed coat removed and cotyledon split • cook quickly and are easily added to soups and tomato sauces	No soak	10 to 15 minutes
CDC Gold	• 5 mm across • thin white seed coat which becomes translucent after cooking to reveal a bright yellow cotyledon • retain light color after cooking and canning	No soak	30 to 40 minutes

Peas

Yellow Peas   Green Peas

Lentils

Laird    Rose

CDC Gold 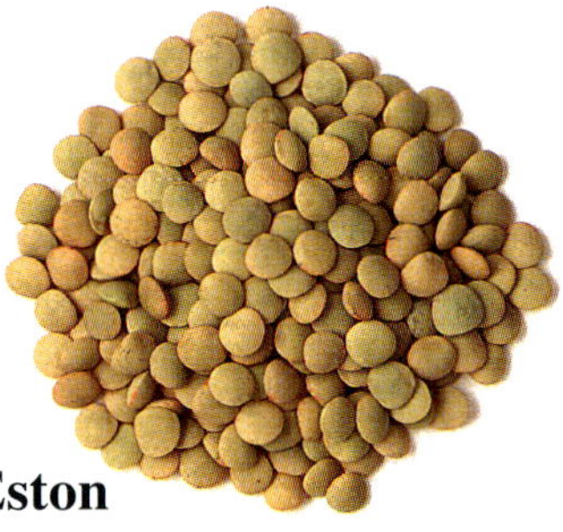   Eston

Beans

Pinto

Red Kidney

Navy (pea) bean

Pink

Black Bean

Red Mexican (small red)

Great Northern

Chickpeas
(Garbanzo beans)

Kabuli

Desi

Beans

Beans are oval-shaped seeds which come in a variety of colors. The major growing areas are Alberta, Manitoba and Ontario. There are a wide variety of beans grown in Canada, but the most popular is the White Pea Bean or Navy Bean. Beans must be soaked before cooking.

Bean	Description	Soaking Method	Cooking Time After Soaking
Great Northern	• large oval-shaped white bean • delicate flavor • great in baked beans or salad	Quick or long	1 to 1½ hours
Pink	• dusty rose color • delicate flavor • easily substituted for other beans	Quick or long	1½ to 2 hours
Pinto	• sand-colored bean with brown freckles • earthy flavor • used extensively in Mexican cooking	Quick or long	1½ to 2 hours
Red Mexican	• small, red oval bean • robust flavor • used in chili, bean salad and Mexican dishes	Quick or long	1½ to 2 hours
Kidney	• white, light or dark red • earth flavor • used in chili and salads	Quick or long	1½ to 2 hours
Navy	• small, white round bean sometimes called white pea bean • traditionally used in baked beans	Quick or long	1 to 1½ hours
Black	• small, black oval bean • nutty flavor • turn a rich brown when cooked • traditionally used in oriental cooking	Quick or long	1 to 1½ hours

Chickpeas (Garbanzo beans)

Chickpeas are light-brown, round, bumpy seeds. They range from pea-size to marble-size depending on variety. Chickpeas require soaking before cooking.

Chickpeas	Description	Soaking Method	Cooking Time
Kabuli	• round, bumpy and light brown • size varies with variety • nutty flavor • often found in salad bars and ethnic cooking	Quick or long	2 to 2½ hours
Desi	• small, round, bumpy and reddish brown • often split, with the seed coat removed – referred to as channa dhal in East Indian cuisine	Quick or long	1½ to 2 hours

No Soak Method:
Lentils and split peas do not require soaking before cooking. Simply wash before use and cook immediately.

Pulse Cookery

Basic Pulse Cooking:

Dried peas, beans and lentils can be cooked in a saucepan on top of the stove, in the oven, microwave, or a slow cooker. Only beans may be cooked in the pressure cooker. Basic cooking principles remain the same regardless of which method is used. Pulses require water or other liquids, oil or fat (to prevent foaming) and seasonings combined with slow cooking. Acid ingredients (such as tomatoes and vinegar) and salt should be added after the softening process has begun, as acids and salt slow down the cooking process.

Alkali, in the form of baking soda, is sometimes suggested to speed up the softening of pulses during cooking, especially if using hard water. Alkali increases water absorption; however, baking soda destroys thiamin found in pulses and may affect texture, making them too soft. Therefore, if using hard water, the amount of baking soda should be regulated to 0.5 mL per 500 mL (⅛ tsp. per 16 oz.) of cooking water. Soft water is preferable for both soaking and cooking.

Cooking Methods

Stove Top Cooking:

To cook on top of the stove, combine soaked or dried pulses with water, oil and seasonings in a heavy saucepan. Be sure to use a large enough saucepan, as pulses double to triple in volume during cooking. Bring to a boil, cover tightly, reduce heat and simmer until tender. Always simmer pulses slowly as cooking too fast can break the seed coats. Cooking times vary according to variety and product end usage. (See chart on pages 17 & 18 for specific times.) At high temperatures, or if using hard water, increase the soaking and cooking time.

Pressure Cooker:

A pressure cooker will cook beans quickly and is a real convenience, but it is not recommended for dried peas or lentils. They tend to foam and clog the vent pipe. Combine dried or soaked beans with water, vegetable oil and seasonings in the cooker; fill no more than half full. Follow the manufacturer's instructions for operation.

Oven Cooking:

Baking in the oven is a slow process, but it is the only way to achieve those great baked pulse dishes. To reduce the cooking length of traditional baked pulses, a combination of stove top followed by oven cooking can be used. Make sure sufficient liquid is added to prevent drying and hardening of the pulse product.

Slow Cooker:

The advantage of a slow cooker is that it cooks all day with no attention; however, it is sometimes hard to cook pulses thoroughly. The low setting is often too low and beans or whole peas in particular may still be hard after 10 hours of cooking. The liquid often evaporates during this time as well. It is necessary to experiment with individual slow cookers to obtain the best results.

Microwave:

This method receives mixed reviews. Some don't recommend it; others do. Either way it takes as long as stove top cooking so there is no time advantage and boil-overs are common. Combine beans or peas and water in a large microwavable casserole. Cover, microwave on High 10 to 15 minutes, or until boiling. Stir, cover, microwave on Medium 25 to 35 minutes, or until fork-tender, stirring every 15 minutes.

Pulse Purée

250	**mL**	**pulses**	**1**	**cup**
625	**mL**	**water or other liquid**	**2½**	**cups**

Wash pulses; soak beans and whole peas as described above. Cover with water. Bring to a boil and reduce heat. Cover and simmer until the pulses are very tender (40-50 minutes for lentils or split peas; 1½-2 hours for beans). Drain, reserving the stock. Blend pulses, adding enough stock to make a purée the consistency of canned pumpkin. As purée forms, stop and mix often until purée is smooth. Makes 500 mL (2 cups). Freezes well.

Sprouting Pulses

Scald a 1 L (1-quart) wide-mouth jar. Wash 50 mL (¼ cup) of lentils or beans and place in the jar. Add 500 mL (2 cups) of lukewarm water. Secure cheesecloth or nylon stocking over the mouth of the jar with a rubber ring, elastic band or jar ring. Let stand 8 hours or overnight. Turn the jar on its side and shake to separate and spread seeds along the side of the jar. Place the jar in a cupboard. Never let the seeds dry out or sit in water too long as this can cause spoilage. The seeds should be rinsed two or three times a day. Keep the jar in a dark place for the first three days, then bring it out and place it in daylight for the last day thus activating the chlorophyll to achieve a nice green color. Lentils take 3-4 days to grow. Eating length is 1-2.5 cm (½-1"). 50 mL (¼ cup) of lentils will yield approximately 175 mL (¾ cup) of sprouts.

Flatulence

"Beans, beans, the musical fruit. . ." Pulses, such as beans, peas, lentils and chickpeas do tend to create gas for some individuals, but no more so than cabbage, broccoli and many other vegetables and fruit. The complex sugars (oligosaccharides) found in pulses cause gas production. These sugars can't be broken down into simple sugars (digested) by human digestive enzymes and therefore pass from the upper intestine into the lower intestine. In the lower intestine, the oligosaccharides are metabolized by bacteria and form carbon dioxide, hydrogen and methane gas.

The soluble fiber found in pulses tends to slow passage through the digestive tract. Therefore, although beans produce gas they don't cause diarrhea.

The human digestive system normally produces gas. About half of the gas is a product of intestinal bacteria while the other half is a result of swallowing air as we eat.

So, how can we reduce the flatulence factor associated with pulses?

1. Cook pulses thoroughly as undercooked starch is harder to digest.

2. Change the soaking water 2 or 3 times during the long soaking processes.

3. When using canned pulses or after using the quick soaking method, rinse beans or peas before cooking.

4. Do not use the soaking liquid to cook the pulses.

5. Regular consumption gives your digestive system a chance for bacteria to adjust to digesting the complex sugars found in pulses and other vegetables and fruits. Start with small amounts, drink lots of water and gradually increase your intake.

6. According to research at Utah State University, germination (sprouting) or fermentation of pulses reduces the amount of complex sugars and consequently the gas production.

7. Adding baking soda (sodium bicarbonate) to cooking water is sometimes recommended. However, it does not affect the complex sugars and therefore does not solve the problem. Baking soda actually destroys some nutrients and can cause the pulses to toughen.

8. Bean flours seem to be easier to digest, plus provide a simple way to add small quantities to nearly everything you cook.

9. There are liquid enzymes on the market which seem to help eliminate gas. They are available in health food stores, pharmacies and most grocery stores. A few drops are added to the gas-producing food before eating.

Nutrient Analysis of Selected Pulses

FOOD	MEASURE	WEIGHT g	WATER %	ENERGY kcal	ENERGY kJ	PROTEIN	CARBOHYDRATES g	FAT g	SFA g	PUFA g	CHOLESTEROL mg	CALCIUM mg	IRON mg	SODIUM mg	POTASSIUM RE	VITAMIN A	THIAMIN mg	RIBOFLAVIN mg	NIACIN mcg	FOLATE	VITAMIN C mg	DIETARY FIBER g
Common white bean, cooked, drained	250 mL	189	63	263	1100	18	47	1	tr	tr	0	170	7.0	11	1060	0	.22	.09	3.9	153	0	8.3
Red kidney, cooked, drained	250 mL	187	67	238	996	16	43	1	tr	tr	0	52	5.5	4	754	0	.30	.11	4.3	242	2	6.7
Chickpeas, boiled, drained	250 mL	173	60	284	1188	15	47	4	tr	2	0	85	5.0	12	504	5	.20	.11	3.4	298	2	6.1
Lentils, cooked, drained	250 mL	209	70	243	1017	19	42	1	tr	tr	0	40	7.0	4	772	2	.35	.15	5.0	378	3	8.4
Peas, split, cooked	250 mL	207	69	244	1021	17	44	1	tr	tr	0	29	2.7	4	750	2	.39	.12	5.1	134	1	4.8

Source: (Health and Welfare Canada (1988), *Nutrient Value of Some Common Foods*)

Glossary of Terms

Al dente:	Briefly cooking pasta until it offers a slight resistance to the bite.
Bake:	Cooking breads, cakes, fruits, casseroles by dry heat, uncovered, in an oven.
Batter:	A thin mixture consisting of a thickener (flour, purée), liquid and other ingredients.
Beat:	Incorporating air into a mixture by using a fork, spoon, whisk or beater.
Blend:	Stirring two or more unlike ingredients together to form a mixture in which separate ingredients are indistinguishable. Preparing ingredients in a blender.
Boil:	Cooking food in liquid at or above the boiling point.
Brown:	Cooking food in a small amount of fat, over moderate heat, until it darkens.
Chop:	Cutting food into small pieces with a knife, blender or food processor.
Combine:	Stirring two or more ingredients together to form a mixture in which separate ingredients are distinguishable.
Cool:	Allowing a mixture to come to room temperature.
Cream:	Beating a mixture with a spoon or mixer until it is soft, smooth and creamy.
Cube:	Cutting food into small cubes 1 cm (½") square.
Dice:	Cutting food into small, uniform pieces.
Dough:	A mixture of liquid and flour which can be handled or kneaded.
Dot:	Scattering bits of fat (butter, margarine) over surface of food.
Dust:	Sprinkling lightly with sugar or flour.
Fold:	Combining one ingredient with another by cutting vertically though mixture with spatula and sliding across the bottom of bowl and up the side, then turning the mixture over.
Fry:	Cooking food over high heat in a small amount of fat.
Glaze:	Coating with a glossy mixture.
Grate:	Rubbing food on a grater (or chopping in a blender or food processor) to produce fine, medium or coarse pieces.
Grease (Oil):	Rubbing surface of pan or dish with vegetable shortening or spraying with vegetable oil to keep food from sticking during baking.
Knead:	Working dough with hands by folding it over on itself, pushing down and away with heels of hands and turning dough one-quarter turn after each folding and pushing motion.

Marinate: Letting food stand in a marinade, a mixture of oil, lemon juice or vinegar and seasonings.

Mince: Chopping food into very fine pieces.

Mix: Stirring two or more like ingredients together to form a mixture which has either distinguishable or indistinguishable ingredients.

Peel: Removing outer covering of food by trimming with knife or vegetable peeler, or pulling off.

Pour: Transferring batter when it flows easily.

Preheat: Heating oven to desired temperature before cooking food.

Pressure Cook: Cooking less tender cuts of meats, vegetables (e.g. beans) in steam underhigh pressure in a pressure cooker.

Purée: Pressing food though a fine sieve or food mill; blending in a blender or food processor to a smooth, thick mixture. Small, measured amounts of liquid may be added to achieve the desired consistency. Pulse purée recipe on page 22.

Roll Out: Lightly rolling dough with a rolling pin to the required shape and thickness.

Sauté: Cooking in a skillet over high heat in a small amount of fat or cooking in a microwave until the food is browned and cooked.

Shred: Cutting food into slivers or slender pieces using a knife or shredder.

Simmer: Cooking food over low heat in a liquid just below the boiling point.

Slice: Cutting food into pieces which are less than 2.5 cm (1 inch) thick.

Sliver: Cutting food into long, thin pieces.

Steam: Cooking food on a rack or in a colander over steaming hot water in a covered pan.

Stir: Mixing ingredients with a circular motion.

Stir-fry: Cooking sliced food quickly, in a wok or skillet.

Strain: Removing food from liquid.

Toss: Mixing food lightly with a lifting motion.

Turn: Pouring a mixture gently into a pan.

Whip: Beating rapidly with a mixer, wire whisk or beater to incorporate air and increase volume.

Gluten-Free

Yield:	375 mL (1½ cups)
Serving Size:	25 mL (2 tbsp.)
Preparation Time:	8 minutes
Pulse Product:	Yellow Split Peas

Nutritional Analysis (per serving)

Calories:	43	
Total Fat:	3	g
Saturated Fat:	1	g
Protein:	2	g
Carbohydrates:	2.5	g
Cholesterol:	7	mg
Sodium:	59	mg
Potassium:	54	mg
Folic Acid:	20	mcg
Total Fiber:	trace	
Soluble:	trace	
Insoluble:	trace	

Diabetic Food Choices

Whole Milk:	½

Dill Spread

Serve this tasty dip with fresh vegetables or crackers*!

175	mL	cooked Yellow Split Peas	¾ cup
125	mL	low-fat yogurt*	½ cup
125	g	low-fat cream cheese, at room temperature	4 oz.
25	mL	light mayonnaise*	2 tbsp.
5	mL	dry crumbled dillweed	½ tsp.
2	mL	lemon juice	½ tsp.
1	mL	salt	¼ tsp.

- In a food processor, combine peas, yogurt, cream cheese, mayonnaise, dillweed, lemon juice and salt. Mix until well blended.
- Cover and refrigerate at least 2 hours.
15 servings

*Gluten-free brand required

Fresh Vegetables Stuffed with Cheesy Lentil Spread

Kids love this spread as a filling for green pepper wedges and celery sticks or as a spread on sandwiches or in pita pockets.

125	g	low-fat cream cheese, at room temperature	4 oz.
125	mL	low-fat cottage cheese	½ cup
5	mL	horseradish sauce	1 tsp.
5	mL	Dijon mustard	1 tsp.
1	mL	Greek seasoning	¼ tsp.
0.5	mL	ground black pepper	⅛ tsp.
250	mL	cooked Eston Lentils	1 cup
50	mL	finely chopped smoked beef OR ham	¼ cup
15	mL	minced radish	1 tbsp.
15	mL	finely chopped green onion	1 tbsp.
		celery sticks	
		cherry tomatoes, tops removed and seeded	
		sweet green pepper, cut in wedges	

- In a food processor, combine cream cheese, cottage cheese, horseradish, mustard, seasoning and pepper. Mix until smooth.
- Stir in lentils, smoked beef, radish and onion.
- Cover and refrigerate 1 hour.
- Fill celery sticks, cherry tomatoes or pepper wedges with 15 mL (1 tbsp.) filling each.

14 servings

Yield:	425 mL (1¾ cups)
Serving Size:	25 mL (2 tbsp.)
Preparation Time:	25 minutes
Pulse Product:	Eston Lentils

Nutritional Analysis
(per serving)

Calories:	48	
Total Fat:	2	g
Saturated Fat:	1	g
Protein:	3.5	g
Carbohydrates:	4.5	g
Cholesterol:	7	mg
Sodium:	85	mg
Potassium:	110	mg
Folic Acid:	14	mcg
Total Fiber:	1.5	g
Soluble:	0.5	g
Insoluble:	1	g

Diabetic Food Choices

Protein:	½
Fruit & Vegetables:	½

Yield:	675 mL (2¾ cups)
Serving Size:	50 mL (¼ cup)
Preparation Time:	15 minutes
Pulse Product:	Yellow Split Peas

Nutritional Analysis
(per serving)

Calories:	69	
Total Fat:	2	g
Saturated Fat:	trace	
Protein:	3.5	g
Carbohydrates:	9	g
Cholesterol:	2	mg
Sodium:	87.5	mg
Potassium:	112	mg
Folic Acid:	56	mcg
Total Fiber:	1.5	g
Soluble:	0.5	g
Insoluble:	1	g

Diabetic Food Choices

Protein:	½
Starch:	½

Hummus

Serve hummus with pita bread or fresh vegetables.*

50	mL	peanut butter**	¼	cup
2	mL	cumin	½	tsp.
2	mL	salt	½	tsp.
2		cloves garlic, minced	2	
25	mL	lemon juice	2	tbsp.
45	mL	hot water	3	tbsp.
5	mL	sesame oil	1	tsp.
625	mL	cooked Yellow Split Peas	2½	cups
		fresh parsley (optional)		
		peanuts (optional)		
		black olives (optional)		

- In a small bowl, combine peanut butter, cumin, salt and garlic.
- Add lemon juice, hot water and sesame oil; mix thoroughly. Purée split peas in food processor or blender; add peanut butter mixture; purée or mix thoroughly.
- Garnish, if desired, with finely chopped parsley, chopped peanuts or sliced black olives.

13 servings

*Not gluten-free
**Gluten-free brand required

Lentil Salsa

A very tasty salsa. If you are in a hurry, simply add cooked lentils to your favorite prepared salsa. The result will taste great and be high in fiber too!

2		medium tomatoes, chopped	2	
250	mL	finely chopped onion	1	cup
114	mL	can green chilies, chopped	4	oz.
250	mL	cooked Eston Lentils	1	cup
25	mL	finely chopped fresh cilantro OR 10 mL (2 tsp.) dry crumbled coriander	2	tbsp.
15	mL	red wine vinegar	1	tbsp.
15	mL	fresh lime juice	1	tbsp.
2		garlic cloves, minced	2	
2	mL	salt	½	tsp.
		crackers*, tortilla chips		

- In a large bowl, combine tomato, onion, chilies, lentils, cilantro, vinegar, lime juice, garlic and salt. Mix well.
- Cover and chill 2 to 3 hours. Serve at room temperature with crackers* or tortilla chips.

12 servings

*Gluten-free brand required

Gluten-Free

Yield:	750 mL (3 cups)
Serving Size:	50 mL (¼ cup)
Preparation Time:	15 minutes
Pulse Product:	Eston Lentils

Nutritional Analysis (per serving)

Calories:	29	
Total Fat:	trace	
Saturated Fat:	trace	
Protein:	2	g
Carbohydrates:	6.5	g
Cholesterol:	0	g
Sodium:	196.5	mg
Potassium:	140.5	mg
Folic Acid:	17	mcg
Total Fiber:	2	g
Soluble:	0.5	g
Insoluble:	1.5	g

Diabetic Food Choices

Fruit & Vegetables: ½

Gluten-Free

Yield:	2 L (8 cups)
Serving Size:	125 mL (½ cup)
Preparation Time:	30 minutes
Pulse Product:	Red Mexican Beans Eston Lentils

Nutritional Analysis
(per serving)

Calories:	109	
Total Fat:	6	g
Saturated Fat:	2.5	g
Protein:	6	g
Carbohydrates:	10	g
Cholesterol:	13.5	mg
Sodium:	374	mg
Potassium:	157	mg
Folic Acid:	28	mcg
Total Fiber:	3	g
Soluble:	1	g
Insoluble:	2	g

Diabetic Food Choices

Protein:	½
Fruit & Vegetables:	1
Fats & Oils:	1

Taco Salad Dip

This dip is great for parties.

375	**mL**	**cooked Red Mexican Beans**	**1½**	**cups**
375	**mL**	**cooked Eston Lentils**	**1½**	**cups**
75	**mL**	**chopped sweet green pepper**	**⅓**	**cup**
250	**mL**	**diced tomato**	**1**	**cup**
50	**mL**	**chopped green onion**	**¼**	**cup**
250	**mL**	**calorie-wise Catalina dressing***	**1**	**cup**
500	**mL**	**shredded lettuce**	**2**	**cups**
500	**mL**	**grated low-fat Cheddar cheese**	**2**	**cups**
		tortilla chips		

- In a bowl, combine beans, lentils, green pepper, tomato, onion and dressing.
- Cover and refrigerate 12 hours.
- Place bean mixture in a serving dish, top with lettuce and cheese.
- Serve immediately with tortilla chips.

16 servings

*Gluten-free brand required

Vegetable Dip in a Pumpernickel Loaf

A low-fat version of a classic dip.

500	mL	Yellow Split Pea purée	2	cups
45	g	vegetable soup mix	1½	oz.
2		green onions, finely chopped	2	
2		garlic cloves, minced	2	
250	mL	finely chopped fresh parsley	1	cup
500	mL	low-fat yogurt	2	cups
1		round loaf of pumpernickel bread vegetable tray crackers	1	

- In a bowl, combine purée, soup mix, onion, garlic, parsley and yogurt.
- Cover and refrigerate 2 hours.
- Cut off the top of the pumpernickel loaf and remove bread inside, leaving a hollow shell. Cut bread removed from loaf into 2.5 cm (1") cubes.
- Fill hollow bread shell with dip.
- Serve with vegetable platter, crackers and cubed bread.

32 servings

Yield:	1 L (4 cups)
Serving Size:	25 mL (2 tbsp.)
Preparation Time:	20 minutes
Pulse Product:	Yellow Split Peas

Nutritional Analysis (per serving)

Calories:	27	
Total Fat:	trace	
Saturated Fat:	trace	
Protein:	2	g
Carbohydrates:	4	g
Cholesterol:	1	mg
Sodium:	30	mg
Potassium:	78.5	mg
Folic Acid:	23	mcg
Total Fiber:	trace	
Soluble:	trace	
Insoluble:	trace	

Diabetic Food Choices

Skim Milk:	½

Gluten-Free

Yield:	625 mL (2 ½ cups)
Serving Size:	50 mL (¼ cup)
Preparation Time:	15 minutes
Pulse Product:	Pink Beans

Nutritional Analysis (per serving)

Calories:	208	
Total Fat:	7	g
Saturated Fat:	2	g
Protein:	9	g
Carbohydrates:	28	g
Cholesterol:	30.5	mg
Sodium:	320.5	mg
Potassium:	186.5	mg
Folic Acid:	30.5	mcg
Total Fiber:	4.5	g
Soluble:	2.5	g
Insoluble:	2	g

Diabetic Food Choices

Protein:	1
Starch:	1
Fruit & Vegetables:	1
Fats & Oils:	1

Pink Bean Shrimp Dip

For a gluten-free alternative to pumpernickel bread*, serve in a bowl with fresh vegetables and gluten-free crackers or rice bread squares.

250	mL	cooked Pink Beans	1	cup
125	g	low-fat cream cheese, at room temperature	4	oz.
125	mL	chopped fresh spinach	½	cup
50	mL	light mayonnaise**	¼	cup
50	mL	low-fat sour cream**	¼	cup
50	mL	chopped fresh parsley	¼	cup
50	mL	chopped green onion	¼	cup
25	mL	lemon juice	2	tbsp.
15	mL	dry crumbled dillweed	1	tbsp.
1		garlic clove, minced	1	
1	mL	ground black pepper	¼	tsp.
113	g	can shrimp, rinsed and drained	4	oz.
1		round loaf pumpernickel bread*	1	

- In a food processor, combine beans, cream cheese, spinach, mayonnaise, sour cream, parsley, onion, lemon juice, dill, garlic and pepper. Blend until smooth.
- Add shrimp. Blend until shrimp is finely chopped but not puréed.
- Cover and refrigerate until ready to serve.
- Cut the top off the bread and remove the bread inside, leaving a hollow shell. Cut the removed bread into 2.5 cm (1") cubes.
- Stuff the pumpernickel loaf with dip and serve with bread cubes and fresh vegetables.

10 servings

*Not gluten-free
**Gluten-free brand required

Toasty Lentil and Salmon Cups

Use leftover bread crusts to make croûtons. Simply cut bread crusts into cubes, toss with canola oil and your favorite herbs. Bake at 100°C (200°F) 30 minutes, or until dry.

375	mL	cooked Eston Lentils	1½	cups
213	g	can salmon, drained	7½	oz.
284	mL	can cream of mushroom soup	10	oz.
1		green onion, thinly sliced	1	
5	mL	freshly squeezed lemon juice	1	tsp.
		pinch of ground black pepper		
20		slices whole-wheat bread	20	

- Preheat oven to 180°C (350°F).
- In a medium bowl, combine lentils, salmon, mushroom soup, onion, lemon juice and pepper.
- Using a 10 cm (4") diameter round cookie cutter, cut centers out of each slice of bread.
- Spray muffin tins lightly with a nonstick vegetable spray. Press bread circles into muffin tins.
- Fill each bread cup with 25 mL (2 tbsp.) of lentil mixture.
- Bake 15 minutes.

20 servings

Yield:	20 toast cups
Serving Size:	1 toast cup
Preparation Time:	40 minutes
Pulse Product:	Eston Lentils

Nutritional Analysis
(per serving)

Calories:	240	
Total Fat:	3	g
Saturated Fat:	1	g
Protein:	20.5	g
Carbohydrates:	45	g
Cholesterol:	4	mg
Sodium:	110	mg
Potassium:	620.5	mg
Folic Acid:	70.5	mcg
Total Fiber:	1	g
Soluble:	trace	
Insoluble:	1	g

Diabetic Food Choices

Protein:	1
Starch:	2
Skim Milk:	1

Yield:	24 shells
Serving Size:	2 shells
Preparation Time:	35 minutes
Pulse Product:	Eston Lentils

Nutritional Analysis
(per serving)

Calories:	235	
Total Fat:	9	g
Saturated Fat:	4	g
Protein:	14	g
Carbohydrates:	25.5	g
Cholesterol:	22	mg
Sodium:	1423.5	mg
Potassium:	186	mg
Folic Acid:	14.5	mcg
Total Fiber:	3	g
Soluble:	1	g
Insoluble:	2	g

Diabetic Food Choices

Protein:	1
Starch:	1
Whole Milk:	1

Salmon and Lentil Stuffed Shells

An inviting beginning to a meal!

24		jumbo pasta shells	24	
375	mL	grated low-fat Cheddar cheese	1½	cups
125	mL	finely chopped sweet red pepper	½	cup
50	mL	finely chopped green onion	¼	cup
50	mL	1% milk	¼	cup
15	mL	lemon juice	1	tbsp.
2	mL	seafood seasoning	½	tsp.
2	mL	salt	½	tsp.
1	mL	ground white pepper	¼	tsp.
1	mL	mace	¼	tsp.
375	mL	cooked Eston Lentils	1½	cups
250	mL	finely chopped smoked salmon	1	cup
75	mL	fine dry bread crumbs	⅓	cup
75	mL	grated Parmesan cheese	⅓	cup
25	mL	margarine, melted	2	tbsp.

- Cook pasta shells according to package instructions, until just tender. Drain, rinse with cold water and drain again. Set aside.
- Preheat oven to 180°C (350°F).
- In a bowl, combine cheese, red pepper, onion, milk, lemon juice, seafood seasoning, salt, pepper and mace. Mix well.
- Stir in lentils and salmon.
- Spoon 25 mL (2 tbsp.) of mixture into shells.
- Place shells in a 22 x 34 cm (9 x 13") baking dish. Add 25 mL (2 tbsp.) water.
- Cover with foil and bake 30 minutes.
- In a bowl, combine crumbs, cheese and margarine. Sprinkle over shells. Bake, uncovered, 5 minutes. Serve hot.

12 servings

Mexican Pink Bean Dip

Serve as a dip with tortilla chips or roll up in a soft tortilla for a spicy lunch.

227	g	ground beef	½ lb.
125	mL	chopped onion	½ cup
35	g	pkg. taco seasoning*	1.3 oz.
50	mL	water	¼ cup
175	mL	taco sauce	¾ cup
50	mL	ketchup*	¼ cup
114	mL	can green chilies, chopped	4 oz.
2	mL	garlic salt	½ tsp.
375	mL	puréed Pink Beans	1½ cups
125	mL	grated Monterey Jack cheese	½ cup

- Preheat oven to 180°C (350°F).
- Brown beef and onion in a skillet, drain off fat.
- Add taco seasoning and water; mix. Add taco sauce, ketchup, chilies, garlic salt and bean purée and mix well.
- Place in a 1.5 L (1½ quart) casserole. Bake, covered, 30 minutes.
- Sprinkle with cheese.
8 servings

*Gluten-free brand required

Gluten-Free

Yield:	1 L (4 cups)
Serving Size:	125 mL (½ cup)
Preparation Time:	30 minutes
Pulse Product:	Pink Beans

Nutritional Analysis (per serving)

Calories:	166	
Total Fat:	9	g
Saturated Fat:	4	g
Protein:	12	g
Carbohydrates:	9.5	g
Cholesterol:	34	mg
Sodium:	527	mg
Potassium:	267.5	mg
Folic Acid:	12.5	mcg
Total Fiber:	2	g
Soluble:	1	g
Insoluble:	1	g

Diabetic Food Choices

Protein:	1½
Starch:	½
Fats & Oil:	½

Yield:	30 fingers
Serving Size:	1 finger
Preparation Time:	25 minutes
Pulse Product:	Rose Lentils

Nutritional Analysis
(per serving)

Calories:	47	
Total Fat:	2	g
Saturated Fat:	1	g
Protein:	2	g
Carbohydrates:	5	g
Cholesterol:	11.5	mg
Sodium:	42	mg
Potassium:	24	mg
Folic Acid:	3	mcg
Total Fiber	trace	
Soluble:	trace	
Insoluble:	trace	

Diabetic Food Choices

2% Milk:	1

Cheddar Crispies

M-M-M-Good! Serve hot out of the oven.

125 mL	margarine	½ cup
250 mL	all-purpose flour	1 cup
250 mL	rice crisp cereal	1 cup
175 mL	grated low-fat Cheddar cheese	¾ cup
175 mL	Rose Lentil purée	¾ cup
1	egg, beaten	1

- Preheat oven to 180° C (350°F).
- In a bowl, cut margarine into flour until mixture resembles coarse oatmeal.
- Stir in cereal, cheese and lentil purée.
- Add egg. Mix well.
- Mold 15 mL (1 tbsp.) amounts into finger shapes. Place on an ungreased baking sheet 5 cm (2") apart. Bake 15 minutes, or until golden.
- Remove from oven and serve immediately.
30 servings.

Lentil Roll-Ups

An elegant appetizer. For variety, try adding 15 mL (1 tbsp.) of low-sodium soy sauce to the filling.

250	mL	cooked Laird Lentils	1	cup
25	mL	grated Parmesan cheese	2	tbsp.
15	mL	finely chopped onion	1	tbsp.
1	mL	dry crumbled oregano	¼	tsp.
1	mL	dry crumbled thyme	¼	tsp.
0.5	mL	ground black pepper	⅛	tsp.
1		garlic clove, minced	1	
454	g	pkg. phyllo pastry	1	lb.
25	mL	canola oil	2	tbsp.

- In a food processor or blender, purée lentils.
- Add cheese, onion, oregano, thyme, pepper and garlic. Mix well.
- Preheat oven to 160°C (325°F).
- Cut individual phyllo pastry sheets into 15 x 20 cm (6 x 8") pieces. Lightly brush with canola oil.
- Spread 5 mL (1 tsp.) filling along one end of pastry sheet and roll over once. Turn in edges of pastry and roll up to make a cigar shape. Repeat this procedure until all of the filling has been used.
- Place filled pastry rolls on a nonstick baking sheet. Bake rolls 15-20 minutes, or until golden brown.

33 servings

Yield:	33 roll-ups
Serving Size:	1 roll-up
Preparation Time:	30 minutes
Pulse Product:	Laird Lentils

Nutritional Analysis (per serving)

Calories:	65	
Total Fat:	2.5	g
Saturated Fat:	0.5	g
Protein:	2	g
Carbohydrates:	9	g
Cholesterol:	1.5	mg
Sodium:	115	mg
Potassium:	26.5	mg
Folic Acid:	3	mcg
Total Fiber:	0.5	g
Soluble:	trace	
Insoluble:	0.5	g

Diabetic Food Choices

Starch:	½
Fats & Oils:	½

Yield:	30 pastries
Serving Size:	2 pastries
Preparation Time:	45 minutes
Pulse Product:	Eston Lentils

Nutritional Analysis
(per serving)

Calories:	88	
Total Fat:	4	g
Saturated Fat:	1.5	g
Protein:	3	g
Carbohydrates.	11.5	g
Cholesterol:	16.5	mg
Sodium:	272	mg
Potassium:	109.5	mg
Folic Acid:	8	mcg
Total Fiber:	2.0	g
Soluble:	0.5	g
Insoluble:	1.5	g

Diabetic Food Choices

Protein:	½
Starch:	½
Fats & Oils:	½

Curried Lentil Pastries

The size of these pastries is great for lunch or a snack. For hors d'oeuvres make a smaller size using 6.5 cm (2½") circles.

7	mL	canola oil	1½	tsp.
15	mL	curry powder	1	tbsp.
375	mL	cooked Eston Lentils	1½	cups
50	mL	tomato paste	¼	cup
175	mL	water	¾	cup
74	g	pkg. French onion soup mix	2½	oz.
125	mL	dry bread crumbs	½	cup
50	mL	currants	¼	cup
540	g	pkg. pie crust mix OR pastry equal to a top and bottom pie crust	19	oz.
1		egg, slightly beaten	1	

- In a skillet over medium heat, cook oil and curry powder for 2 minutes.
- Add lentils, tomato paste, water, onion soup mix, bread crumbs and currants. Cook, stirring constantly, 5 minutes. Cool.
- Prepare pie crust according to package directions. Cut pastry into 9 cm (3½") circles. Brush circles with lightly beaten egg.
- Preheat oven to 200°C (400°F).
- Place 15 mL (1 tbsp.) of filling in the middle of each circle, leaving an edge of at least 2.5 cm (1") all around. Fold 2 edges together and pinch edges to seal. Place pastries on an ungreased cookie sheet, seam side up.
- Brush with egg and bake 25-30 minutes, or until pastry is golden brown.

15 servings

Saucy Lentil Cocktail Balls

Use the sauce as a dip or coating for the cocktail balls. Salsa also makes an excellent dip!

175	mL	chili sauce	¾	cup
125	mL	grape jelly	½	cup
125	mL	Eston Lentil purée	½	cup
175	mL	dried bread crumbs	¾	cup
50	mL	finely diced onion	¼	cup
5	mL	dried crumbled parsley	1	tsp.
25	mL	all-purpose flour	2	tbsp.
2	mL	salt	½	tsp.
2	mL	Worcestershire sauce	½	tsp.
1	mL	ground black pepper	¼	tsp.
1		egg, slightly beaten	1	
50	mL	canola oil	¼	cup

- In a saucepan, combine chili sauce and grape jelly. Melt over low heat. Set aside.
- In a bowl, combine lentil purée, bread crumbs, onion, parsley, flour, salt, Worcestershire sauce, pepper and egg. Mix thoroughly.
- Measure 15 mL (1 tbsp.) portions of mixture and roll into ball shapes.
- In a skillet, heat oil. Add lentil balls, cooking until all sides are well browned. Reheat sauce.
- Place browned lentil balls into the sauce, completely coating them.
- Serve immediately.

7 servings

Yield:	28 balls
Serving Size:	4 balls
Preparation Time:	30 minutes
Pulse Product:	Eston Lentils

Nutritional Analysis
(per serving)

Calories:	152	
Total Fat:	1.5	g
Saturated Fat:	0.5	g
Protein:	4	g
Carbohydrates:	32	g
Cholesterol:	40	mg
Sodium:	249.5	mg
Potassium:	245.5	mg
Folic Acid:	11.5	mcg
Total Fiber:	1.5	g
Soluble:	0.5	g
Insoluble:	1	g

Diabetic Food Choices

Starch:	2

Yield:	20 wedges
Serving Size:	1 wedge
Preparation Time:	45 minutes
Pulse Product:	Red Mexican Beans

Nutritional Analysis
(per serving)

Calories:	110	
Total Fat:	7	g
Saturated Fat:	3.5	g
Protein:	4	g
Carbohydrates:	7.5	g
Cholesterol:	25	mg
Sodium:	169	mg
Potassium:	87	mg
Folic Acid:	5.5	mcg
Total Fiber:	1	g
Soluble:	0.5	g
Insoluble:	0.5	g

Diabetic Food Choices

Protein:	½
Starch:	½
Fats & Oils:	½

Red Mexican Bean Pie

For a wonderful summer variation of this pie, mix sour cream and cream cheese until smooth. Spread over bean purée. Omit remaining ingredients. Bake 8 minutes. Cool. Top with fruit.

235	g	pkg. refrigerated crescent roll dough	8	oz.
300	mL	Red Mexican Bean purée	1¼	cups
250	mL	low-fat sour cream	1	cup
125	g	low-fat cream cheese	4	oz.
25	mL	finely sliced green onion	2	tbsp.
15	mL	chopped fresh parsley	1	tbsp.
2	mL	dry crumbled oregano	½	tsp.
2	mL	dry crumbled basil	½	tsp.
1	mL	salt	¼	tsp.
125	mL	halved sweet red pepper rings	½	cup
250	mL	quartered, sliced, unpeeled cucumber	1	cup
50	mL	sliced black olives	¼	cup
250	mL	drained canned shrimp	1	cup

- Preheat oven to 190°C (375°F).
- Separate dough into triangles. Place on pizza pan with points towards center to form a circle. Press to seal seams and cover pan.
- Bake 7 minutes, or until slightly browned.
- Spread bean purée over crust.
- In a bowl, mix sour cream and cream cheese until smooth. Mix in onion, parsley, oregano, basil and salt. Spread over bean purée.
- Arrange red pepper, cucumber, olives and shrimp on top. Bake 10 minutes, or until heated through.
- Remove; cut into 20 wedges. Serve warm.
20 servings

Lentil Zucchini Boats

A contest winner!

2	green onions, finely chopped	2	
1	garlic clove, minced	1	
15 mL	canola oil	1	tbsp.
250 mL	sliced fresh mushrooms	1	cup
625 mL	cooked Eston Lentils	2½	cups
25 mL	French onion soup mix	2	tbsp.
5 mL	salt	1	tsp.
50 mL	water	¼	cup
3	medium zucchini	3	
3	sweet green peppers	3	
25 mL	calorie-wise Italian salad dressing	2	tbsp.
50 mL	grated Parmesan cheese	¼	cup

- Preheat oven to 180°C (350°F).
- In a skillet, sauté onion and garlic in oil. Add mushrooms and lentils.
- In a bowl, dissolve soup mix and salt in water and add to lentil mixture. Keep warm while preparing the other vegetables.
- Halve zucchini and peppers and scoop out centers. Brush 2 mL (½ tsp.) Italian dressing on the inside of each vegetable half.
- Fill zucchini and peppers with lentil mixture. Place on a nonstick cookie sheet. Sprinkle with Parmesan cheese.
- Bake 15-20 minutes, or until tender.

12 servings

Filling Yield:	1 L (4 cups)
Serving Size:	1 vegetable half stuffed with 75 mL (⅓ cup) of filling
Preparation Time:	30 minutes
Pulse Product:	Eston Lentils

Nutritional Analysis
(per serving)

Calories:	84	
Total Fat:	4	g
Saturated Fat:	0.5	g
Protein:	4.5	g
Carbohydrates:	11	g
Cholesterol:	3	mg
Sodium:	316	mg
Potassium:	193	mg
Folic Acid:	17	mcg
Total Fiber:	4	g
Soluble:	1	g
Insoluble:	3	g

Diabetic Food Choices

Protein:	½
Fruit & Vegetables:	1
Fats & Oils:	½

S O U P S

Gluten-Free

Yield:	2.75 L (11 cups)
Serving Size:	250 mL (1 cup)
Preparation Time:	30 minutes
Pulse Product:	Eston Lentils

Nutritional Analysis
(per serving)

Calories:	189	
Total Fat:	5	g
Saturated Fat:	1.5	g
Protein:	11	g
Carbohydrates:	27	g
Cholesterol:	6	mg
Sodium:	242	mg
Potassium:	539.5	mg
Folic Acid:	13	mcg
Total Fiber:	4.5	g
Soluble:	1.5	g
Insoluble:	3	g

Diabetic Food Choices

Protein:	1
Fruit & Vegetable:	2

Vegetable Soup

A simple soup which requires a 1 hour simmering time.

25 mL	canola oil	2 tbsp.
750 mL	coarsely chopped carrot	3 cups
500 mL	chopped onion	2 cups
175 mL	chopped celery	¾ cup
5 mL	dry crumbled marjoram	1 tsp.
2 mL	ground thyme	½ tsp.
1.75 L	water	7 cups
540 mL	can tomatoes, chopped	19 oz.
375 mL	Eston Lentils	1½ cups
15 mL	tomato paste*	1 tbsp.
3x6.5 g	pkg. light chicken bouillon*	3x¼ oz.
15 mL	dry crumbled parsley	1 tbsp.
2 mL	salt	½ tsp.
2 mL	ground black pepper	½ tsp.
250 mL	grated low fat mozzarella cheese	1 cup

- In a large saucepan or Dutch oven, heat oil.
- Add carrot, onion, celery, marjoram and thyme. Sauté until onion is translucent.
- Add water, tomatoes, lentils, tomato paste and bouillon. Bring to a boil; reduce heat; cover and simmer 1 hour.
- Add parsley, salt and pepper. Simmer 5 minutes. Top with mozzarella cheese.

11 servings

*Gluten-free brand required

Hearty Lentil Stew

Lentils are the base for this outstanding soup.

25	mL	canola oil	2 tbsp.
250	mL	chopped onion	1 cup
250	mL	chopped sweet green pepper	1 cup
250	mL	chopped sweet red pepper	1 cup
875	mL	water	3½ cups
796	mL	can tomatoes	28 oz.
375	mL	Eston Lentils	1½ cups
250	mL	chopped carrot	1 cup
50	mL	chopped pimiento	¼ cup
10	mL	salt	2 tsp.
5	mL	dry crumbled oregano	1 tsp.
7	mL	dry crumbled dillweed	1½ tsp.
1	mL	ground black pepper	¼ tsp.
2		garlic cloves, minced	2

- In a large saucepan or Dutch oven, heat oil. Add onion and peppers. Cook until tender.
- Add water, tomatoes, lentils, carrot, pimiento, salt, oregano, dillweed, pepper and garlic. Mix well. Bring the stew to a boil. Reduce heat; cover and simmer 45 minutes, or until lentils are tender.

8 servings

Gluten-Free

Yield:	2 L (8 cups)
Serving Size:	250 mL (1 cup)
Preparation Time:	40 minutes
Pulse Product:	Eston Lentils

Nutritional Analysis
(per serving)

Calories:	115	
Total Fat:	4	g
Saturated Fat:	trace	
Protein:	5	g
Carbohydrates:	18	g
Cholesterol:	0	mg
Sodium:	633	mg
Potassium:	501.5	mg
Folic Acid:	23	mcg
Total Fiber:	8	g
Soluble:	2	g
Insoluble:	6	g

Diabetic Food Choices

Protein:	½
Starch:	1
Fats & Oils:	½

Yield:	3 L (12 cups)
Serving Size:	250 mL (1 cup)
Preparation Time:	25 minutes
Pulse Product:	Navy Beans

Nutritional Analysis
(per serving)

Calories:	158	
Total Fat:	3	g
Saturated Fat:	1	g
Protein:	8	g
Carbohydrates:	26	g
Cholesterol:	4.5	mg
Sodium:	411	mg
Potassium:	492	mg
Folic Acid:	30	mcg
Total Fiber:	7.5	g
Soluble:	3	g
Insoluble:	4.5	g

Diabetic Food Choices

Protein:	1
Fruit & Vegetable:	2

Bean Chowder

This soup will become a family favorite.

250	mL	chopped onion	1	cup
250	mL	chopped celery	1	cup
1		garlic clove, minced	1	
50	mL	margarine	¼	cup
50	mL	all-purpose flour	¼	cup
1		vegetable bouillon cube	1	
675	mL	water	2¾	cups
750	mL	2 % milk	3	cups
1.25	L	cooked Navy Beans	5	cups
540	mL	can tomatoes	19	oz.
341	mL	can whole kernel corn	12	oz.
398	mL	can cut green beans	14	oz.
0.5	mL	ground black pepper	⅛	tsp.
5	mL	hickory smoke salt	1	tsp.

- In a large saucepan or Dutch oven, sauté onion, celery and garlic in margarine until soft.
- Stir in flour.
- Add vegetable bouillon cube, water and milk, stirring to dissolve cube.
- Add beans, tomatoes, corn and green beans. Heat to a gentle boil.
- Add pepper and hickory smoke salt.
12 servings

Southwestern Pinto Bean and Corn Soup

*A **hearty, easy-to-prepare** soup!*

500	**mL**	**Pinto Beans, soaked overnight**	**2 cups**
1.5	**L**	**water**	**6 cups**
6x6.5	**g**	**pkg.light instant chicken bouillon***	**6x¼ oz.**
5	**mL**	**dry crumbled thyme**	**1 tsp.**
796	**mL**	**can tomatoes, chopped**	**28 oz.**
125	**mL**	**chopped celery**	**½ cup**
398	**mL**	**can cream-style corn***	**14 oz.**
1	**mL**	**ground black pepper (optional)**	**½ tsp.**

- In a large saucepan or Dutch oven, combine beans, water, bouillon and thyme.
- Bring to a boil, reduce heat, cover and simmer 1½ hours, or until beans are tender.
- Remove 250 mL (1 cup) beans and mash with fork. Return mashed beans to saucepan or Dutch oven.
- Add tomatoes, celery, corn and pepper.
- Bring mixture to a boil, reduce heat, cover and simmer 30 minutes, or until celery is tender.

12 servings

*Gluten-free brand required

Gluten-Free

Yield:	3 L (12 cups)
Serving Size:	250 mL (1 cup)
Preparation Time:	15 minutes
Pulse Product:	Pinto Beans

Nutritional Analysis (per serving)

Calories:	161	
Total Fat:	1	g
Saturated Fat:	trace	
Protein:	8	g
Carbohydrates:	32	g
Cholesterol:	0	mg
Sodium:	214	mg
Potassium:	610.5	mg
Folic Acid:	92	mcg
Total Fiber:	6	g
Soluble:	2.5	g
Insoluble:	3.5	g

Diabetic Food Choices

Protein:	½
Starch:	2

Yield:	1.25 L	(5 cups)
Serving Size:	250 mL	(1 cup)
Preparation Time:	30 minutes	
Pulse Product:	Pinto Beans	

Nutritional Analysis
(per serving)

Calories:	328	
Total Fat:	20	g
Saturated Fat:	4	g
Protein:	16	g
Carbohydrates:	22	g
Cholesterol:	20	g
Sodium:	725	mg
Potassium:	670	mg
Folic Acid:	37.5	mcg
Total Fiber:	4.5	g
Soluble:	2	g
Insoluble:	2.5	g

Diabetic Food Choices

Protein:	2
Starch:	1
Fruit & Vegetables:	½
Fats & Oils:	3

Green Chili and Bean Soup

Hot! Hot! Hot! Wonderful! Wonderful! Wonderful!

1.5		onions, chopped	1½
3		garlic cloves, minced	3
25	mL	canola oil	2 tbsp.
10	mL	paprika	2 tsp.
1	L	chicken broth*	4 cups
398	mL	can tomatoes, chopped	14 oz.
114	mL	can green jalapeño chilies	4 oz.
250	mL	cubed potato	1 cup
2	mL	cumin	½ tsp.
250	mL	cooked Pinto Beans	1 cup
2	mL	salt	½ tsp.
1	mL	ground black pepper	¼ tsp.
175	mL	grated Monterey Jack cheese	¾ cup

- In a large saucepan or Dutch oven, sauté onion and garlic in oil until brown.
- Add paprika and brown 2 minutes more, stirring constantly.
- Add chicken broth, tomatoes, green chilies, potato, cumin, beans, salt and pepper.
- Simmer 30-45 minutes, or until potatoes are tender.
- Divide cheese among 5 soup bowls. Ladle soup into bowls. Serve steaming hot.

5 servings

*Gluten-free brand required

Lentil Soup with Hot Peppers

Protect your hands with rubber gloves when preparing chili peppers. Chili peppers may be peeled with a vegetable peeler, just as you would peel a carrot. Skins may also be removed by roasting.

25	mL	canola oil	2	tbsp.
250	mL	chopped onion	1	cup
750	mL	cooked Eston Lentils	3	cups
500	mL	chopped tomatoes	2	cups
375	mL	chopped carrot	1½	cups
4		garlic cloves, minced	4	
15	mL	finely chopped fresh red chili pepper	1	tbsp.
1.5	L	water	6	cups
2	mL	salt	½	tsp.
10		whole black peppercorns	10	
2		vegetable bouillon cubes**	2	

- In a large saucepan or Dutch oven, heat oil and sauté onion 2 minutes.
- Add lentils, tomatoes, carrot and garlic. Mix well. Sauté 2 minutes.
- Add chili pepper and cook 2 minutes.
- Add water, salt, peppercorns and bouillon cubes. Bring the soup to a boil; reduce heat and simmer until vegetables are tender.

10 servings

*Roast sweet or hot peppers on a cookie sheet in a 200°C (400°F) oven for 25-30 minutes, turning peppers once. Remove peppers from the oven and put them in a paper bag or cover them to trap the heat and moisture. Let peppers cool and the skin will peel off easily.

**Gluten-free brand required

Gluten-Free

Yield:	2.5 L (10 cups)
Serving Size:	250 mL (1 cup)
Preparation Time:	25 minutes
Pulse Product:	Eston Lentils

Nutritional Analysis (per serving)

Calories:	103	
Total Fat:	3	g
Saturated Fat:	trace	
Protein:	6	g
Carbohydrates:	17	g
Cholesterol:	trace	
Sodium:	308.5	mg
Potassium:	312	mg
Folic Acid:	23.5	mcg
Total Fiber:	6	g
Soluble:	1.5	g
Insoluble:	4.5	g

Diabetic Food Choices

Protein:	½
Starch:	1
Fats & Oils:	½

Yield:	2.75 L (11 cups)
Serving Size:	250 mL (1 cup)
Preparation Time:	20 minutes
Pulse Product:	Great Northern Beans

Nutritional Analysis
(per serving)

Calories:	72	
Total Fat:	3	g
Saturated Fat:	trace	
Protein:	2	g
Carbohydrates:	10	g
Cholesterol:	0	mg
Sodium:	261	mg
Potassium:	236	mg
Folic Acid:	10	mcg
Total Fiber:	2.5	g
Soluble:	1	g
Insoluble:	1.5	g

Diabetic Food Choices

Starch:	½
Fats & Oils:	½

Great Northern Minestrone Soup

This is a meal in itself! For gluten-free use rice instead of orzo and a gluten-free brand of bouillon.*

25	mL	canola oil	2 tbsp.
250	mL	chopped celery	1 cup
250	mL	sliced green beans	1 cup
250	mL	shredded cabbage	1 cup
175	mL	finely chopped onion	¾ cup
1.75	L	boiling water	7 cups
540	mL	can tomatoes	19 oz.
250	mL	Great Northern Beans, soaked overnight	1 cup
125	mL	orzo pasta	½ cup
3x6.5 g		pkg. light chicken bouillon	3x¼ oz.
5	mL	dry crumbled oregano	1 tsp.
5	mL	dry crumbled basil	1 tsp.
5	mL	Bon Appétit seasoning**	1 tsp.
5	mL	salt	1 tsp.
2	mL	ground black pepper	½ tsp.
1		bay leaf	1

- In a large saucepan or Dutch oven, heat oil.
- Add celery, green beans, cabbage and onion. Sauté until onion is translucent.
- Add boiling water, tomatoes, beans, orzo, chicken bouillon, oregano, basil, Bon Appétit, salt, pepper and bay leaf.
- Bring to a boil, cover, reduce heat and simmer 75 minutes, or until the beans are tender. Remove the bay leaf.

11 servings

*Orzo is a rice shaped pasta. Use as a side dish or in soups and stews.

**Omit if you are allergic to MSG, and increase amounts of other seasonings.

Bean Borscht

Just like Grandma's!

1		medium onion, chopped	1	
500	mL	shredded cabbage	2	cups
15	mL	margarine	1	tbsp.
2	L	beef broth*	8	cups
500	mL	grated cooked beets	2	cups
500	mL	cooked Pink Beans	2	cups
15	mL	lemon juice	1	tbsp.
15	mL	chopped fresh dillweed	1	tbsp.
		OR 5 mL (1 tsp.) dry crumbled dillweed		
5	mL	granulated sugar	1	tsp.
		freshly ground black pepper to taste		

- In a large saucepan or Dutch oven, sauté onion and cabbage in margarine until soft, but not brown.
- Add beef broth and beets. Simmer 20 minutes.
- Add beans, lemon juice, dillweed, sugar and pepper. Simmer 10 minutes.

10 servings

*Gluten-free brand required

Gluten-Free

Yield:	2.5 L (10 cups)
Serving Size:	250 mL (1 cup)
Preparation Time:	25 minutes
Pulse Product:	Pink Beans

Nutritional Analysis (per serving)

Calories:	189	
Total Fat:	10	g
Saturated Fat:	trace	g
Protein:	10	g
Carbohydrates:	15	g
Cholesterol:	2.5	mg
Sodium:	333.5	mg
Potassium:	375.5	mg
Folic Acid:	24	mcg
Total Fiber:	5	g
Soluble:	1.5	g
Insoluble:	3.5	g

Diabetic Food Choices

Protein:	1
Fruit & Vegetables:	1
Fats & Oils:	1½

Yield:	3 L
	(12 cups)
Serving Size:	250 mL
	(1 cup)
Preparation Time:	40 minutes
Pulse Product:	Laird Lentils

Nutritional Analysis
(per serving)

Calories:	208	
Total Fat:	10	g
Saturated Fat:	trace	
Protein:	12	g
Carbohydrates:	19	g
Cholesterol:	3	mg
Sodium:	144	mg
Potassium:	451	mg
Folic Acid:	14	mcg
Total Fiber:	1.5	g
Soluble:	1	g
Insoluble:	0.5	g

Diabetic Food Choices

Protein:	1½
Fruit & Vegetable:	1½
Fats & Oils:	1

Lentil Soup with Yogurt

Lentils are superb soup-makers! This recipe combines two Middle Eastern staples, lentils and yogurt.

25	mL	canola oil	2	tbsp.
2		large onions, grated	2	
0.5		small cabbage, grated	½	
2		medium carrots, grated	2	
250	mL	Laird Lentils	1	cup
2		medium parsnips, diced	2	
2		celery stalks, chopped	2	
2		garlic cloves, minced	2	
2		bay leaves	2	
5	mL	dill seed	1	tsp.
50	mL	tomato paste	¼	cup
2	L	chicken stock*	8	cups
		salt and ground black pepper to taste		
		low-fat yogurt*		

Optional spices:

7	mL	marjoram	1½	tsp.
2	mL	savory	½	tsp.

- In a large saucepan or Dutch oven, heat oil.
- Add onion, cabbage and carrot. Sauté 20 minutes, stirring often.
- Add lentils, parsnip, celery, garlic, bay leaves, dill seed, tomato paste and stock. Add salt and pepper to taste.
- Cover and simmer 2-2½ hours. Remove bay leaves.
- To serve, ladle hot soup into bowls, garnish with a dollop of yogurt.

12 servings

*Gluten-free brand required

Lentil Chickpea Stew

Chickpeas and almonds add crunch to this favorite.

3		medium onions, chopped	3	
1		garlic clove, minced	1	
5	mL	canola oil	1	tsp.
4		celery stalks, sliced	4	
250	mL	chopped carrot	1	cup
5	mL	cumin	1	tsp.
1	mL	cardamom	¼	tsp.
1	mL	cinnamon	¼	tsp.
125	mL	Gold Lentils	½	cup
750	mL	chicken broth*	3	cups
250	mL	water	1	cup
125	mL	cooked Chickpeas	½	cup
125	mL	slivered almonds	½	cup

- In a saucepan or Dutch oven, sauté onion and garlic in oil until onion is tender.
- Add celery, carrot, cumin, cardamom, cinnamon, lentils, chicken broth and water.
- Cover and simmer 45 minutes, or until lentils are tender.
- Stir in Chickpeas and almonds and cook until heated through.

6 servings

*Gluten-free brand required

Gluten-Free

Yield:	1.5 L (6 cups)
Serving Size:	250 mL (1 cup)
Preparation Time:	30 minutes
Pulse Product:	Gold Lentils Chickpeas

Nutritional Analysis
(per serving)

Calories:	238	
Total Fat:	13.5	g
Saturated Fat:	0.5	g
Protein:	12	g
Carbohydrates:	21	g
Cholesterol:	2.5	mg
Sodium:	115	mg
Potassium:	495	mg
Folic Acid:	33	mcg
Total Fiber:	6	g
Soluble:	2	g
Insoluble:	4	g

Diabetic Food Choices

Protein:	1
Starch:	1
Fats & Oils:	2

Gluten-Free

Yield:	2 L (8 cups)
Serving Size:	250 mL (1 cup)
Preparation Time:	20 minutes
Pulse Product:	Yellow Split Peas

Nutritional Analysis
(per serving)

Calories:	279	
Total Fat:	12	g
Saturated Fat:	0.5	g
Protein:	15	g
Carbohydrates:	30	g
Cholesterol:	2.5	mg
Sodium:	191	mg
Potassium:	529	mg
Folic Acid:	9	mcg
Total Fiber:	3	g
Soluble:	1	g
Insoluble:	2	g

Diabetic Food Choices

Protein:	2
Starch:	1
Fruit & Vegetables:	1
Fats & Oils:	1

Curried Split Pea Soup

A tasty version of an old classic!

15	mL	margarine	1	tbsp.
125	mL	chopped onion	½	cup
25	mL	chopped celery leaves	2	tbsp.
1		garlic clove, minced	1	
5	mL	curry powder*	1	tsp.
150	mL	Yellow Split Peas, washed and drained	⅔	cup
750	mL	chicken stock*	3	cups
125	mL	grated carrot	½	cup
125	mL	grated apple	½	cup
		low-fat yogurt* to taste		

- In a small saucepan, over medium heat, melt margarine.
- Add onion, celery leaves and garlic; sauté 3 minutes, or until onion is soft.
- Add curry; stir for 1 minute.
- In a large saucepan or Dutch oven, combine peas and chicken stock. Cover and bring to a boil. Reduce heat and simmer 15 minutes.
- Add onion mixture, carrot and apple, simmer 10 minutes, or until peas are tender.
- Serve with a spoonful of yogurt.

4 servings

*Gluten-free brand required

Classic Split Pea Soup

If you prefer, use whole peas for this soup. Soak them overnight and increase the cooking time slightly.

250	mL	Yellow Split Peas	1 cup
1	L	water	4 cups
4x6.5	g	pkg. light instant chicken bouillon*	4x¼ oz.
125	mL	chopped onion	½ cup
175	mL	diced carrot	¾ cup
175	mL	diced potato	¾ cup
125	mL	diced cooked ham*	½ cup
1		bay leaf	1
0.5	mL	ground black pepper	⅛ tsp.

- In a large saucepan or Dutch oven, combine peas, water, bouillon, onion, carrot, potato, ham and bay leaf.
- Bring to a boil; reduce heat; cover and simmer, stirring occasionally, 45-60 minutes, or until peas are tender and soup has thickened. Remove the bay leaf.
- Just before serving add pepper.

5 servings

*Gluten-free brand required

Gluten-Free

Yield:	1.25 L (5 cups)
Serving Size:	250 mL (1 cup)
Preparation Time:	15 minutes
Pulse Product:	Yellow Split Peas

Nutritional Analysis (per serving)

Calories:	222	
Total Fat:	3	g
Saturated Fat:	1	g
Protein:	13.5	g
Carbohydrates:	36	g
Cholesterol:	6.5	mg
Sodium:	246.5	mg
Potassium:	615	mg
Folic Acid:	11.5	mcg
Total Fiber:	3.5	g
Soluble:	1.5	g
Insoluble:	2	g

Diabetic Food Choices

| Protein: | 1½ |
| Starch: | 2 |

Gluten-Free

Yield: 2 L
               (8 cups)

Serving Size: 250 mL
               (1 cup)

Preparation Time: 20 minutes

Pulse Product: Green Split
                   Peas

Nutritional Analysis
(per serving)

Calories:	417	
Total Fat:	16	g
Saturated Fat:	1.5	g
Protein:	28	g
Carbohydrates:	42	g
Cholesterol:	12.5	mg
Sodium:	743	mg
Potassium:	849.5	mg
Folic Acid:	14	mcg
Total Fiber:	4.5	g
Soluble:	2	g
Insoluble:	2.5	g

Diabetic Food Choices

Protein:	3
Starch:	2
Fruit & Vegetables:	½
Fats & Oils:	2

Split Pea Soup

For a new taste sensation, add a touch of vinegar before serving.

1	**large ham bone**	**1**	
2.25 L	**water**	**9**	**cups**
1	**bay leaf**	**1**	
550 mL	**Green Split Peas**	**2¼**	**cups**
500 mL	**cooked chopped ham***	**2**	**cups**
250 mL	**chopped onion**	**1**	**cup**
250 mL	**chopped carrot**	**1**	**cup**
125 mL	**chopped celery**	**½**	**cup**
1 mL	**ground black pepper**	**¼**	**tsp.**
5 mL	**salt**	**1**	**tsp.**
	vinegar (optional)		

- In a large saucepan or Dutch oven, simmer ham bone, water and bay leaf for 30 minutes.
- Add peas, cover and simmer 1 hour, or until peas are tender.
- Remove the ham bone and add chopped ham, onion, carrot, celery, pepper and salt.
- Cover and simmer until vegetables are tender, about 15 minutes. Remove the bay leaf.
- If you wish, add a touch of vinegar to each serving.

8 servings

*Gluten-free brand required

Italian Split Pea Soup

A savory soup!

75	mL	sun-dried tomatoes	⅓	cup
125	mL	warm water	½	cup
250	mL	sliced celery	1	cup
500	mL	water	2	cups
6		slices pepperoni,* chopped	6	
375	mL	Green Split Pea purée	1½	cups
250	mL	cooked Yellow Split Peas	1	cup
2		garlic cloves, minced	2	
5	mL	dry crumbled oregano	1	tsp.
1		light beef bouillon cube* Parmesan cheese (optional)	1	

- Soak sun-dried tomatoes in warm water 5 minutes.
- In a large saucepan, simmer celery in water 10 minutes. Add pepperoni, purée and peas.
- Remove tomatoes from water. Reserve the water. Chop tomatoes and add with reserved water to split pea mixture.
- Add garlic, oregano and bouillon cube. Bring to a boil, cover, and simmer 10 minutes.
- Spoon into bowls, sprinkle with Parmesan cheese.

8 servings

*Gluten-free brand required

Gluten-Free

Yield:	1.5 L (6 cups)
Serving Size:	175 mL (¾ cup)
Preparation Time:	30 minutes
Pulse Product:	Green Split Peas Yellow Split Peas

Nutritional Analysis
(per serving)

Calories:	107	
Total Fat:	3	g
Saturated Fat:	1	g
Protein:	7	g
Carbohydrates:	14	g
Cholesterol:	5	mg
Sodium:	285	mg
Potassium:	296	mg
Folic Acid:	5	mcg
Total Fiber:	2.5	g
Soluble:	1	g
Insoluble:	1.5	g

Diabetic Food Choices

Protein:	1
Fruit & Vegetables:	1

Yield:	4 L
	(16 cups)
Serving Size:	250 mL
	(1 cup)
Preparation Time:	30 minutes
Pulse Product:	Chickpeas
	Pink Beans

Nutritional Analysis
(per serving)

Calories:	255	
Total Fat:	19	g
Saturated Fat:	8	g
Protein:	9.5	g
Carbohydrates:	12	g
Cholesterol:	32.5	mg
Sodium:	581	mg
Potassium:	376	mg
Folic Acid:	27	mcg
Total Fiber:	2.5	g
Soluble:	1	g
Insoluble:	1.5	g

Diabetic Food Choices

Protein:	1½
Starch:	½
Fats & Oils:	3

Corleone Luncheon Soup

Fork or spoon !?!

680	g	mild Italian sausage* or farmer sausage*	1½	lbs.
1		large onion, chopped	1	
796	mL	can tomatoes, chopped	28	oz.
10		large mushrooms, chopped	10	
2x284	mL	cans beef broth*	2x10	oz.
625	mL	water	2½	cups
1		garlic clove, minced	1	
2	mL	dry crumbled basil	½	tsp.
540	mL	can Chickpeas, drained	19	oz.
250	mL	cooked Pink Beans	1	cup
4		small zucchini, quartered and sliced	4	
		grated Parmesan cheese to taste		
		dash of dry crumbled parsley		

- In a large saucepan or Dutch oven, cook sausage until lightly brown. Drain off excess grease. Cut sausage into 1 cm (½") chunks.
- Add onion, tomatoes, mushrooms, beef broth, water, garlic, basil, Chickpeas, beans and zucchini.
- Bring to a boil. Reduce heat and simmer 12 minutes, or until zucchini slices are tender but still intact.
- Serve with a garnish of grated Parmesan cheese and parsley.

16 servings

*Gluten-free brand required

Lentil Soup and Dumplings

Serve in heated, large, rimmed soup bowls.
(see dumpling recipe on following page)

2		chicken backs (for stock)	2	
1	L	water	4	cups
2	mL	salt	½	tsp.
1		light chicken bouillon cube	1	
250	mL	Laird Lentils	1	cup
125	mL	shredded carrot	½	cup
125	mL	sliced parsnip*	½	cup
250	mL	sliced celery	1	cup
1		medium onion, chopped	1	
2		garlic cloves, minced	2	
25	mL	canola oil	2	tbsp.
375	mL	2% milk	1½	cups
15	mL	finely chopped fresh dillweed	1	tbsp.

- Wash chicken backs. In a large saucepan or Dutch oven, add chicken backs to water, bring to a boil. Skim top of soup; when clear, cover and simmer 1½ hours.
- Remove backs, add salt, bouillon cube and lentils. Bring to a boil; cook 2 minutes, stirring occasionally. Remove from heat.
- In a medium skillet, sauté carrot, parsnip, celery, onion, and garlic in oil.
- Stir sautéed vegetables into lentil mixture. Bring to a boil; reduce heat, cover and simmer 30 minutes, or until lentils are tender. Add dumplings (see following recipe). Cook 15 minutes more.
- Stir in milk and dill. Continue cooking until soup is hot but not boiling.
- Ladle soup and 4 dumplings into each bowl.

6 servings

*Substitute 250 mL (1 cup) carrots for parsnips, if desired.

Yield:	1.75 L (7 cups)
Serving Size:	250 mL (1 cup)
Preparation Time:	25 minutes
Pulse Product:	Laird Lentils

Nutritional Analysis
(per serving)

Calories:	410	
Total Fat:	21.5	g
Saturated Fat:	4	g
Protein:	23	g
Carbohydrates:	32	g
Cholesterol:	72.5	mg
Sodium:	846	mg
Potassium:	680	mg
Folic Acid:	18	mcg
Total Fiber:	4	g
Soluble:	1	g
Insoluble:	3	g

Diabetic Food Choices

Protein:	3
Starch:	½
Fruit & Vegetables:	1½
Fats & Oils:	2

Ham and Cheese Dumplings

Yield: 24 dumplings

Serving Size: 4 dumplings

Preparation Time: 15 minutes

45	mL	margarine	3 tbsp.
175	mL	grated low-fat Cheddar cheese	¾ cup
50	mL	shredded ham OR luncheon meat	¼ cup
50	mL	all-purpose flour	¼ cup
2	mL	dry mustard	½ tsp.
1		egg	1

- In a small bowl, combine margarine, cheese, meat, flour and mustard. Stir in egg.
- Dust hands with flour and shape rounded teaspoons (8-10 mL) of dumpling mixture into 2 cm (1") balls. Drop dumplings into hot soup. Cover and simmer 15 minutes, or until dumplings are cooked.

Helen's Pulse Stew

A tribute to pulses!

125	mL	Pink Beans, soaked overnight	½ cup
125	mL	Great Northern Beans, soaked overnight	½ cup
125	mL	Yellow Split Peas	½ cup
125	mL	Green Split Peas	½ cup
125	mL	Laird Lentils	½ cup
750	mL	water	3 cups
500	mL	diced cooked ham	2 cups
284	mL	can light chicken broth	10 oz.
796	mL	can tomatoes	28 oz.
250	mL	chopped carrot	1 cup
250	mL	chopped onion	1 cup
125	mL	chopped celery	½ cup
2		garlic cloves, minced	2
5	mL	chili powder	1 tsp.
2	mL	salt	½ tsp.
1	mL	ground black pepper	¼ tsp.

- Drain beans. In a large saucepan or Dutch oven, combine beans, peas and lentils. Cover with water.
- Add ham and chicken broth. Bring the lentil mixture to a boil. Cover and reduce heat. Simmer 30 minutes.
- Add tomatoes, carrot, onion, celery, garlic and chili powder. Cover and simmer 30 minutes, or until beans are tender.
- Add salt and pepper before serving.

8 servings

Yield:	2 L (8 cups)
Serving Size:	250 mL (1 cup)
Preparation Time:	30 minutes
Pulse Product:	Pink Beans Great Northern Beans Yellow Split Peas Green Split Peas Laird Lentils

Nutritional Analysis
(per serving)

Calories:	265	
Total Fat:	6	g
Saturated Fat:	2	g
Protein:	19	g
Carbohydrates:	36	g
Cholesterol:	15	mg
Sodium:	820.5	mg
Potassium:	859	mg
Folic Acid:	20.5	mcg
Total Fiber:	4	g
Soluble:	2	g
Insoluble:	2	g

Diabetic Food Choices

Protein:	2
Starch:	1½
Fruit & Vegetables:	½

Yield:	2 L (8 cups)
Serving Size:	250 mL (1 cup)
Preparation Time:	35 minutes
Pulse Product:	Pinto Beans

Nutritional Analysis
(per serving)

Calories:	190	
Total Fat:	8.5	g
Saturated Fat:	2	g
Protein:	11.5	g
Carbohydrates:	18	g
Cholesterol:	11	mg
Sodium:	720	mg
Potassium:	523	mg
Folic Acid:	43	mcg
Total Fiber:	5	g
Soluble:	2	g
Insoluble:	3	g

Diabetic Food Choices

Protein:	1
Starch:	1
Fats & Oils:	1

Hearty Ham and Bean Soup

Microwave instructions make this a quick and easy supper!

15	mL	margarine	1 tbsp.
1		medium onion, chopped	1
1		garlic clove, minced	1
1		sweet green pepper, diced	1
125	mL	diced celery	½ cup
25	mL	all-purpose flour	2 tbsp.
500	mL	chicken stock	2 cups
540	mL	can tomatoes	19 oz.
500	mL	cooked Pinto Beans	2 cups
5	mL	dry crumbled basil	1 tsp.
5	mL	salt	1 tsp.
500	mL	cooked, diced ham	2 cups
50	mL	grated Parmesan cheese	¼ cup

- In a 3 L (3-quart) microwave-safe casserole, microwave margarine on high for 1 minute.
- Add onion, garlic, green pepper and celery. Microwave on high 3 minutes. Stir in flour and stock, blending well.
- Drain and chop tomatoes, reserving juice. Add tomatoes and beans to casserole along with their juices, basil and salt.
- Cover with waxed paper and microwave on high 10 minutes.
- Stir in ham and microwave, uncovered, 4 more minutes.
- Sprinkle each serving with grated cheese.
8 servings

Lentil Sausage Stew

A meal in a bowl!

15	mL	canola oil	1 tbsp.
1		sweet red pepper, chopped	1
375	mL	Laird Lentils	1½ cups
454	g	Ukrainian OR Polish sausage*, cut in 1 cm (½") thick rounds	1 lb.
750	mL	chicken broth*	3 cups
540	mL	can tomatoes	19 oz.
2	mL	dry crumbled thyme	½ tsp.
250	mL	sliced green onion	1 cup
250	mL	sliced zucchini	1 cup
125	mL	finely chopped fresh parsley	½ cup
25	mL	white vinegar	2 tbsp.

- In a large saucepan or Dutch oven, over medium-high heat, heat oil.
- Add peppers and cook 5 minutes, stirring often.
- Stir in lentils, sausage, broth, tomatoes and thyme. Bring to a boil, cover, reduce heat and simmer 30-40 minutes, or until lentils are almost tender, stirring once or twice.
- Stir in green onions and zucchini; simmer, covered, 10 minutes, until vegetables are tender and liquid has slightly thickened.
- Just before serving, add parsley and vinegar.

10 servings

*Gluten-free brand required

Gluten-Free

Yield:	2.5 L (10 cups)
Serving Size:	250 mL (1 cup)
Preparation Time:	25 minutes
Pulse Product:	Laird Lentils

Nutritional Analysis (per serving)

Calories:	263	
Total Fat:	19.5	g
Saturated Fat:	6.5	g
Protein:	12	g
Carbohydrates:	12	g
Cholesterol:	26	mg
Sodium:	684.5	mg
Potassium:	399.5	mg
Folic Acid:	18	mcg
Total Fiber:	4	g
Soluble:	1	g
Insoluble:	3	g

Diabetic Food Choices

Protein:	1½
Fruit & Vegetables:	1
Fats & Oils:	3

Gluten-Free

Yield:	2.5 L (10 cups)
Serving Size:	250 mL (1 cup)
Preparation Time:	45 minutes
Pulse Product:	Laird Lentils

Nutritional Analysis
(per serving)

Calories:	241	
Total Fat:	7	g
Saturated Fat:	2	g
Protein:	27	g
Carbohydrates:	18	g
Cholesterol:	69	mg
Sodium:	567	mg
Potassium:	728	mg
Folic Acid:	24.5	mcg
Total Fiber:	4	g
Soluble:	1.5	g
Insoluble:	2.5	g

Diabetic Food Choices

Protein:	3
Fruit & Vegetables:	1½

Sopa De Pollo à la Mexicana

Chicken and vegetable soup. Spice it up with green chilies if you like it hot!

1-1.5	kg	frying chicken, cut up, skin and fat removed	2½-3 lbs.
2	L	water	8 cups
0.5		medium onion, sliced	½
4		celery stalks, sliced	4
5	mL	salt	1 tsp.
		pinch of ground black pepper	
150	mL	Laird Lentils	⅔ cup
540	mL	can tomatoes, chopped	19 oz.
3		medium carrots, thinly sliced	3
1		medium onion, chopped	1
2		chicken bouillon cubes*	2
1		small zucchini, thinly sliced	1
250	mL	frozen peas	1 cup
1		small avocado, peeled and sliced	1

- In a Dutch oven, combine chicken, water, onion, celery, salt and pepper. Simmer, covered, 2 hours, until chicken is tender.
- Remove chicken from broth; set aside to cool. Strain broth, discarding vegetables; return broth to Dutch oven.
- Add lentils, tomatoes, carrots, onion and bouillon cubes. Simmer, covered, 30 minutes, or until the carrots are tender.
- When chicken is cool, cube and add to broth with the zucchini and peas.
- Cover and simmer 10-15 minutes longer, or until vegetables are tender.
- Garnish with avocado slices.

10 servings

*Gluten-free brand required

Pinto Bean Hamburger Chowder

This is a change from the conventional chunky seafood chowders. Serve with fresh bread. A comforting meal on a cold night.

500	mL	Pinto Beans, soaked overnight	2	cups
4	L	water	16	cups
1		bay leaf	1	
15	mL	salt	1	tbsp.
1	L	cubed potato	4	cups
250	mL	chopped carrot	1	cup
250	mL	chopped celery	1	cup
125	mL	pearl barley	½	cup
375	mL	chopped onion	1½	cups
50	mL	margarine	¼	cup
454	g	lean ground beef	1	lb.
796	mL	can tomatoes	28	oz.
5	mL	ground black pepper	1	tsp.

- Drain and rinse beans.
- In a large saucepan or Dutch oven, combine beans, water and bay leaf, cover and bring to a boil. Reduce heat and simmer 45 minutes, until beans are just tender.
- Add salt, potato, carrot, celery and barley. Simmer until barley is tender, about 30 minutes.
- In a skillet, sauté onion in margarine. Add beef and brown. Drain off excess fat. Add tomatoes, cook 10 minutes, stirring frequently.
- Add beef mixture to bean mixture when barley is tender. Add pepper. Bring chowder mixture to a boil.
- Remove bay leaf before serving.
  17 servings

Yield:	4.25 L (17 cups)
Serving Size:	250 mL (1 cup)
Preparation Time:	50 minutes
Pulse Product:	Pinto Beans

Nutritional Analysis (per serving)

Calories:	210	
Total Fat:	6	g
Saturated Fat:	2	g
Protein:	12	g
Carbohydrates:	27	g
Cholesterol:	20	mg
Sodium:	474	mg
Potassium:	694	mg
Folic Acid:	64	mcg
Total Fiber:	5	g
Soluble:	2	g
Insoluble:	3	g

Diabetic Food Choices

Protein:	1½
Starch:	1
Fruit & Vegetables:	1

S A L A D S

Gluten-Free

Yield:	500 mL (2 cups)
Serving Size:	125 mL (½ cup)
Preparation Time:	20 minutes
Pulse Product:	Red Mexican Beans Great Northern Beans

Nutritional Analysis
(per serving)

Calories:	226	
Total Fat:	7.5	g
Saturated Fat:	0.5	g
Protein:	7	g
Carbohydrates:	35	g
Cholesterol:	0	mg
Sodium:	14	mg
Potassium:	626.5	mg
Folic Acid:	104.5	mcg
Total Fiber:	6.5	g
Soluble:	3	g
Insoluble:	3.5	g

Diabetic Food Choices

Protein:	½
Starch:	2
Fats & Oils:	1

Pictured on page 53.

Bean and Melon Salad

Wonderful to serve on a hot summer day.

250	mL	cooked Red Mexican Beans	1 cup
250	mL	cooked Great Northern Beans	1 cup
250	mL	cantaloupe melon balls	1 cup
250	mL	honeydew melon balls	1 cup
125	mL	diced sweet red pepper	½ cup
1		green onion, sliced	1

Lemon Mustard Dressing:

25	mL	canola oil	2 tbsp.
25	mL	lemon juice	2 tbsp.
25	mL	granulated sugar	2 tbsp.
2	mL	dry mustard	½ tsp.

- In a bowl, combine beans, cantaloupe, honeydew, pepper and onion.
- In a small container with lid, combine oil, lemon juice, sugar and dry mustard. Shake well.
- Pour dressing over beans and melon mixture. Toss lightly.
- Serve on a bed of lettuce or in melon shells.
4 servings

Oriental Lentil-Rice Salad

An unusual salad with lots of flavor and crunch.

Lemon Soy Dressing:

125 mL	canola oil	½	cup
25 mL	cider vinegar	2	tbsp.
25 mL	lemon juice	2	tbsp.
25 mL	sodium-reduced soy sauce*	2	tbsp.
2 mL	salt	½	tsp.
500 mL	cooked Eston Lentils	2	cups
500 mL	cooked converted rice	2	cups
284 mL	can sliced mushrooms, drained	10	oz.
250 mL	sliced celery	1	cup
284 mL	can mandarin oranges, drained	10	oz.
25 mL	sliced green onion	2	tbsp.
125 mL	slivered almonds	½	cup

- In a container with a tight-fitting lid, combine oil, vinegar, lemon juice, soy sauce and salt. Shake well.
- Combine lentils, rice and mushrooms.
- Pour dressing over lentil mixture, cover and chill at least 1 hour.
- Just before serving, add celery, mandarin oranges, onion and almonds.

12 servings

*Gluten-free brand required

Gluten-Free

Yield:	1.5 L (6 cups)
Serving Size:	125 mL (½ cup)
Preparation Time:	15 minutes
Pulse Product:	Eston Lentils

Nutritional Analysis (per serving)

Calories:	158	
Total Fat:	8	g
Saturated Fat:	1	g
Protein:	5.5	g
Carbohydrates:	19	g
Cholesterol:	0	mg
Sodium:	278	mg
Potassium:	283.5	mg
Folic Acid:	39	mcg
Total Fiber:	4	g
Soluble:	1	g
Insoluble:	3	g

Diabetic Food Choices

Protein:	1
Starch:	1
Fats & Oils:	1½

Pictured on page 53.

Yield:	2 L (8 cups)
Serving Size:	125 mL (½ cup)
Preparation Time:	20 minutes
Pulse Product:	Yellow Split Peas

Nutritional Analysis
(per serving)

Calories:	179	
Total Fat:	12	g
Saturated Fat:	1	g
Protein:	5.5	g
Carbohydrates:	13	g
Cholesterol:	16	mg
Sodium:	368.5	mg
Potassium:	183	mg
Folic Acid:	5.5	mcg
Total Fiber:	1	g
Soluble:	0.5	g
Insoluble:	0.5	g

Diabetic Food Choices

Protein:	1
Starch:	½
Fruit & Vegetables:	½
Fats & Oils:	2

Oriental Pea Salad

***Everyone loves a salad —
especially this one!***

500	**mL**	**cooked (just tender), drained Yellow Split Peas**	**2**	**cups**
375	**mL**	**diced cooked chicken**	**1½**	**cups**
300	**mL**	**cooked white rice**	**1¼**	**cups**
175	**mL**	**fresh bean sprouts**	**¾**	**cup**
175	**mL**	**shredded carrot**	**¾**	**cup**
175	**mL**	**sliced celery**	**¾**	**cup**
125	**mL**	**sliced green onion**	**½**	**cup**
50	**mL**	**diced sweet green pepper**	**¼**	**cup**
250	**mL**	**Zesty Italian dressing**	**1**	**cup**
250	**mL**	**chow mein noodles**	**1**	**cup**

- In a bowl, combine peas, chicken, rice, sprouts, carrot, celery, onion and pepper. Toss lightly.
- Add dressing and toss lightly until evenly coated. Cover and refrigerate 4 hours.
- Place salad in a serving bowl and top with chow mein noodles.

16 servings

Lentil Confetti Salad

When dressing is added to warm lentils and rice, they absorb the flavors more quickly.

250	mL	cooked Laird Lentils, still warm	1	cup
250	mL	cooked white rice, still warm	1	cup
125	mL	bottled Italian dressing*	½	cup
1		large tomato, seeded and diced	1	
1		celery stalk, diced	1	
1		green onion, diced	1	
50	mL	diced sweet green pepper	¼	cup
6		large tomatoes	6	
6		lettuce leaves	6	
		chopped fresh parsley for garnish		

- Combine warm lentils and rice, pour the Italian dressing over the lentil mixture and refrigerate until cool.
- Add diced tomato, celery, onion and pepper. Mix well.
- With base end of the tomato up, slice each tomato into 8 wedges without cutting through the stem end. (4 vertical cuts which cross each other in the center.) Place each tomato on a lettuce leaf. Spread wedges apart slightly. Fill tomato with lentil salad. Garnish with parsley before serving.

6 servings

*Gluten-free brand required

Gluten-Free

Yield:	750 mL (3 cups)
Serving Size:	125 mL (½ cup)
Preparation Time:	30 minutes
Pulse Product:	Laird Lentils

Nutritional Analysis (per serving)

Calories:	221	
Total Fat:	14	g
Saturated Fat:	1	g
Protein:	5	g
Carbohydrates:	22	g
Cholesterol:	13.5	mg
Sodium:	430	mg
Potassium:	504	mg
Folic Acid:	50	mcg
Total Fiber:	5	g
Soluble:	1.5	g
Insoluble:	3.5	g

Diabetic Food Choices

Protein:	½
Starch:	1
Fats & Oils:	2

Mediterranean Salad, page 82
condiments in side dish

Yield:	1 L (4 cups)
Serving Size:	250 mL (1 cup)
Preparation Time:	10 minutes
Pulse Product:	Laird Lentils

Nutritional Analysis (per serving)

Calories:	223	
Total Fat:	7	g
Saturated Fat:	0.5	g
Protein:	9.5	g
Carbohydrates:	36.5	g
Cholesterol:	0	mg
Sodium:	68	mg
Potassium:	413	mg
Folic Acid:	70	mcg
Total Fiber:	9.5	g
Soluble:	2	g
Insoluble:	7.5	g

Diabetic Food Choices

Protein:	1
Starch:	2
Fats & Oils:	1

Lentil and Brown Rice Salad

Tuck this salad into pita bread or roll it up in a tortilla.*

500	**mL**	**cooked Laird Lentils**	**2**	**cups**
125	**mL**	**cooked brown rice**	**½**	**cup**
250	**mL**	**halved cherry tomatoes**	**1**	**cup**
50	**mL**	**chopped green onion**	**¼**	**cup**
45	**mL**	**cider vinegar**	**3**	**tbsp.**
25	**mL**	**canola oil**	**2**	**tbsp.**
10	**mL**	**honey**	**2**	**tsp.**
2	**mL**	**dry crumbled oregano**	**½**	**tsp.**

- In a bowl, combine lentils, rice, tomatoes, onion, vinegar, oil, honey and oregano. Toss lightly.
- Cover and chill before serving.

4 servings

*Not gluten-free

Lentil Vegetarian Salad

Rice, lentils and cheese combine to make a complete protein in this salad.

White Wine Dressing:

50 mL	light mayonnaise*	¼	cup
50 mL	white wine vinegar	¼	cup
15 mL	dry mustard	1	tbsp.
2 mL	granulated sugar	½	tsp.
2 mL	salt	½	tsp.
2 mL	ground black pepper	½	tsp.
250 mL	cooked brown rice, still hot	1	cup
250 mL	cooked Laird Lentils, still hot	1	cup
500 mL	broccoli florets	2	cups
500 mL	sliced fresh mushrooms	2	cups
1	tomato, chopped	1	
125 mL	coarsely grated carrot	½	cup
125 mL	cubed Swiss cheese	½	cup
125 mL	cubed low-fat Cheddar cheese	½	cup

- In a bowl, combine mayonnaise, vinegar, mustard, sugar, salt and pepper. Stir well.
- Pour dressing over hot cooked rice and lentils. Stir well; set aside to cool.
- Place broccoli florets in a vegetable steamer. Steam 5 minutes, or until tender-crisp.
- Add broccoli, mushrooms, tomato, carrot and cheeses to rice/lentil mixture. Toss to mix thoroughly.
- Cover and chill at least 2 hours.

6 servings

*Gluten-free brand required

Gluten-Free

Yield:	1.5 L (6 cups)
Serving Size:	250 mL (1 cup)
Preparation Time:	25 minutes
Pulse Product:	Laird Lentils

Nutritional Analysis (per serving)

Calories:	231	
Total Fat:	10	g
Saturated Fat:	1	g
Protein:	9	g
Carbohydrates:	30	g
Cholesterol:	14	mg
Sodium:	537	mg
Potassium:	454	mg
Folic Acid:	62	mcg
Total Fiber:	4	g
Soluble:	1	g
Insoluble:	3	g

Diabetic Food Choices

Protein:	1
Starch:	½
Fruit & Vegetables:	1
Fats & Oils:	½

Bean & Barley Salad

Beans and barley — what a great combination! Remember to wear rubber gloves when handling jalapeño peppers.

750	mL	water	3 cups
125	mL	pearl barley	½ cup
540	mL	can Chickpeas, rinsed and drained	19 oz.
250	mL	cooked Pink Beans	1 cup
250	mL	cooked Great Northern Beans	1 cup
50	mL	chopped green onion	¼ cup
50	mL	chopped fresh parsley	¼ cup
2		jalapeño peppers, chopped	2

Red Wine Dressing:

75	mL	red wine vinegar	⅓ cup
5	mL	salt	1 tsp.
2	mL	ground black pepper	½ tsp.
2	mL	cumin	½ tsp.
1		garlic clove, minced	1
75	mL	canola oil	⅓ cup

- In a saucepan, bring water to a boil. Reduce heat and add barley. Cook, covered, 40 minutes, or until tender-firm. Remove from heat. Drain. Rinse with cold water. Drain again.
- In a serving bowl, combine barley, Chickpeas, beans, onion, parsley and peppers.
- In a separate bowl, combine vinegar, salt, pepper, cumin and garlic. Whisk in oil until evenly mixed. Add to bean mixture. Toss gently.
- Serve immediately at room temperature. (May be stored in a covered container in refrigerator 24 hours).

10 servings

Dressing Yield:	125 mL (½ cup)
Salad Yield:	1.25 L (5 cups)
Serving Size:	125 mL (½ cup)
Preparation Time:	25 minutes
Pulse Product:	Pink Beans Great Northern Beans Chickpeas

Nutritional Analysis (per serving)

Calories:	179	
Total Fat:	7	g
Saturated Fat:	0.5	g
Protein:	6	g
Carbohydrates:	23	g
Cholesterol:	2	mg
Sodium:	198	mg
Potassium:	247.5	mg
Folic Acid:	46.5	mcg
Total Fiber:	5	g
Soluble:	2	g
Insoluble:	3	g

Diabetic Food Choices

Protein:	½
Starch:	1
Fats & Oils:	1

Some Like It Hot

Pulses and pasta are perfect partners!

250	mL	elbow macaroni	1 cup
250	mL	cooked Red Mexican Beans	1 cup
250	mL	chopped celery	1 cup
125	mL	coarsely shredded carrot	½ cup
25	mL	finely sliced green onion	2 tbsp.

Mayonnaise Chili Dressing:

150	mL	light mayonnaise	⅔ cup
25	mL	1% milk	2 tbsp.
5	mL	chili powder	1 tsp.
2	mL	salt	½ tsp.
1	mL	ground dry oregano	¼ tsp.
1	mL	garlic powder	¼ tsp.
		dash of hot red pepper sauce	

- Cook macaroni according to package directions. Drain and rinse with cold water. Drain again.
- Combine macaroni, beans, celery, carrot, and onion.
- In a separate bowl, combine mayonnaise, milk, chili powder, salt, oregano, garlic powder and pepper sauce. Mix well.
- Add dressing to macaroni mixture and gently mix. Cover and refrigerate several hours. If desired, just before serving spoon salad into a lettuce-lined bowl.

10 servings

Dressing Yield:	175 mL (¾ cup)
Salad Yield:	1.25 L (5 cups)
Serving Size:	125 mL (½ cup)
Preparation Time:	20 minutes
Pulse Product:	Red Mexican Beans

Nutritional Analysis (per serving)

Calories:	105	
Total Fat:	7	g
Saturated Fat:	trace	
Protein:	2	g
Carbohydrates:	9	g
Cholesterol:	9	mg
Sodium:	191.5	mg
Potassium:	126	mg
Folic Acid:	11	mcg
Total Fiber:	2	g
Soluble:	1	g
Insoluble:	1	g

Diabetic Food Choices

Starch:	½
Fats & Oils:	1

Chickpea-Pasta Salad

Chickpeas make the difference in this salad.

750 mL	**cooked corkscrew pasta, drained and cooled**	**3 cups**
398 mL	**can Chickpeas, rinsed and drained**	**14 oz.**
125 mL	**chopped celery**	**½ cup**
125 mL	**coarsely shredded carrot**	**½ cup**
75 mL	**chopped sweet green pepper**	**⅓ cup**
25 mL	**finely sliced green onion**	**2 tbsp.**

Dijon Dressing:

50 mL	**white vinegar**	**¼ cup**
25 mL	**light mayonnaise**	**2 tbsp.**
15 mL	**canola oil**	**1 tbsp.**
10 mL	**Dijon-style mustard**	**2 tsp.**
1 mL	**salt**	**¼ tsp.**
1 mL	**ground black pepper**	**¼ tsp.**
1	**medium tomato, cut into wedges**	**1**

- In a large bowl, combine pasta, Chickpeas, celery, carrot, pepper and onion. Toss lightly until evenly mixed.
- In a separate bowl, whisk together vinegar, mayonnaise, oil, mustard, salt and pepper until well blended.
- Add dressing to Chickpea mixture. Toss lightly until evenly coated. Cover and refrigerate 2 hours. Just prior to serving, garnish with tomato wedges.

14 servings

Dressing Yield:	125 mL (½ cup)
Salad Yield:	1.75 L (7 cups)
Serving Size:	125 mL (½ cup)
Preparation Time:	25 minutes
Pulse product:	Chickpeas

Nutritional Analysis (per serving)

Calories:	79	
Total Fat:	2	g
Saturated Fat:	trace	
Protein:	3	g
Carbohydrates:	12.5	g
Cholesterol:	2	mg
Sodium:	57	mg
Potassium:	134	mg
Folic Acid:	38.5	mcg
Total Fiber:	2	
Soluble:	1	
Insoluble:	1	

Diabetic Food Choices

Protein:	½
Fruit & Vegetables:	1

Guacamole Salad

A unique chickpea salad.

Peppery Avocado Dressing:

125 mL	peeled, chopped avocado	½ cup
125 mL	1% milk	½ cup
50 mL	lemon juice	¼ cup
25 mL	low-fat sour cream	2 tbsp.
1 mL	salt	¼ tsp.
1 mL	chili powder	¼ tsp.
1 mL	Worcestershire sauce	¼ tsp.
	dash of hot red pepper sauce	
1	garlic clove, minced	1
1 L	shredded leaf lettuce	4 cups
500 mL	shredded spinach	2 cups
398 mL	can Chickpeas, rinsed and drained	14 oz.
398 mL	can hearts of palm, drained, sliced	14 oz.
250 mL	chopped sweet red pepper	1 cup

- In a food processor, purée avocado, milk, lemon juice, sour cream, salt, chili powder, Worcestershire sauce, pepper sauce and garlic.
- In a large salad bowl, combine lettuce, spinach, Chickpeas and hearts of palm. Toss lightly.
- Serve salad in individual bowls.
- Top with avocado dressing and garnish with red pepper.

18 servings

Dressing Yield:	250 mL (1 cup)
Salad Yield:	2.25 L (9 cups)
Serving Size:	125 mL (½ cup)
Preparation Time:	35 minutes
Pulse Product:	Chickpeas

**Nutritional Analysis
(per serving)**

Calories:	52	
Total Fat:	2	g
Saturated Fat:	trace	
Protein:	2	g
Carbohydrates:	7.5	g
Cholesterol:	2	mg
Sodium:	81.5	mg
Potassium:	195	mg
Folic Acid:	57	mcg
Total Fiber:	1.5	g
Soluble:	0.5	g
Insoluble:	1	g

Diabetic Food Choices

Starch:	½

Yield:	2.5 L	
	(10 cups)	
Serving Size:	125 mL	
	(½ cup)	
Preparation Time:	30 minutes	
Pulse Product:	Laird Lentils	
	Chickpeas	

Nutritional Analysis
(per serving)

Calories:	96	
Total Fat:	1	g
Saturated Fat:	trace	
Protein:	5.5	g
Carbohydrates:	18	g
Cholesterol:	1	mg
Sodium:	29	mg
Potassium:	296	mg
Folic Acid:	69	mcg
Total Fiber:	5	g
Soluble:	1.5	g
Insoluble:	3.5	g

Diabetic Food Choices

Protein:	½
Starch:	1

Marinated Lentil Salad

A great salad to have on hand. It keeps well in the refrigerator for one week.

1	L	cooked Laird Lentils	4	cups
540	mL	Chickpeas, rinsed, drained	19	oz.
250	mL	finely chopped cauliflower	1	cup
250	mL	finely chopped sweet green pepper	1	cup
10		carrots, diced	10	
1		large onion, finely chopped	1	

Tomato Marinade:

284	mL	can tomato soup	10	oz.
125	mL	granulated sugar	½	cup
125	mL	canola oil	½	cup
250	mL	white vinegar	1	cup
7	mL	garlic powder	1½	tsp.
5	mL	dry mustard	1	tsp.
2	mL	ground black pepper	½	tsp.

- In a large bowl, combine lentils, Chickpeas, cauliflower, green pepper, carrot and onion. Toss lightly. Set aside.
- In a large saucepan or Dutch oven, combine tomato soup, sugar, oil, vinegar, garlic powder, dry mustard and pepper. Simmer 1 minute. Cool completely.
- Pour marinade over vegetables. Refrigerate at least 6 hours; drain off marinade before serving.

20 servings

Greek Lentil Salad

Serve in a pita pocket or as a salad.

250	mL	Eston Lentils	1	cup
750	mL	water	3	cups
1		bay leaf	1	
250	mL	chopped cucumber	1	cup
125	mL	chopped onion	½	cup
2		medium tomatoes, chopped	2	
0.5		large sweet yellow pepper, chopped	½	
250	mL	chopped cauliflower	1	cup
125	mL	chopped fresh parsley	½	cup
112	g	feta cheese, crumbled	4	oz.
125	mL	sliced black olives	½	cup

Greek Salad Dressing:

0.5		lemon, juice of	½	
2	mL	grated lemon peel	½	tsp.
15	mL	red wine vinegar	1	tbsp.
2		garlic cloves, minced	2	
2	mL	salt	½	tsp.
2	mL	granulated sugar	½	tsp.
10	mL	dry crumbled oregano	2	tsp.
2	mL	dry crumbled mint	½	tsp.
1	mL	dry crumbled basil	¼	tsp.
5	mL	Greek seasoning	1	tsp.
75	mL	canola oil	⅓	cup

- Rinse and drain lentils. In a saucepan, combine lentils, water and bay leaf. Bring to a boil; cover, reduce heat and simmer 15 minutes. Drain; remove bay leaf and cool.
- Combine lentils and remaining salad ingredients.
- In a blender, combine all dressing ingredients; blend.
- Toss lentil mixture lightly with dressing.
- Chill for several hours or overnight.
  16 servings

Yield:	2 L (8 cups)
Serving Size:	125 mL (½ cup)
Preparation Time:	40 minutes
Pulse Product:	Eston Lentils

Nutritional Analysis
(per serving)

Calories:	137	
Total Fat:	8.5	g
Saturated Fat:	2	g
Protein:	5	g
Carbohydrates:	11	g
Cholesterol:	5	mg
Sodium:	652.5	mg
Potassium:	228	mg
Folic Acid:	10.5	mcg
Total Fiber:	2	g
Soluble:	0.5	g
Insoluble:	1.5	g

Diabetic Food Choices

Protein:	½
Fruit & Vegetables:	1
Fats & Oils:	1

80

Yield:	1.5 L (6 cups)
Serving Size:	125 mL (½ cup)
Preparation Time:	35 minutes
Pulse Product:	Laird Lentils

Nutritional Analysis
(per serving)

Calories:	184	
Total Fat:	10	g
Saturated Fat:	1	g
Protein:	7	g
Carbohydrates:	19	g
Cholesterol:	0	g
Sodium:	930.5	mg
Potassium:	343	mg
Folic Acid:	13	mcg
Total Fiber:	4	g
Soluble:	1	g
Insoluble:	3	g

Diabetic Food Choices

Protein:	1
Fruit & Vegetables:	1½
Fats & Oils:	2

Lemon Greek Salad

To roast peppers, broil 5 cm (2") from broiler until skins begin to bubble, turn to broil the other side. Cool and peel off the charred skin.

375	mL	Laird Lentils, rinsed, drained	1½	cups
750	mL	water	3	cups
0.5		small onion, diced	½	
1		bay leaf	1	
1		garlic clove, minced	1	
2	mL	salt	½	tsp.
1		medium carrot, diced	1	
2		sweet red peppers, roasted, chopped	2	
1		large tomato, chopped	1	
250	mL	chopped cucumber	1	cup
125	mL	chopped black olives	½	cup
250	mL	chopped cauliflower	1	cup
50	mL	chopped fresh parsley	¼	cup

Lemon Dressing:

1	mL	ground black pepper	¼	tsp.
10	mL	red wine vinegar	2	tsp.
1		large lemon, juice of and grated peel	1	
1	mL	paprika	¼	tsp.
		pinch of cayenne pepper		
1		garlic clove, minced	1	
2	mL	salt	½	tsp.
75	mL	canola oil	⅓	cup

- In a Dutch oven, combine lentils, water, onion, bay leaf and garlic. Bring to a boil, cover, reduce heat and simmer 30 minutes. Drain and cool. Remove bay leaf. Add salt.
- In a large bowl, combine lentils and remaining vegetables. Chill before serving.
- In a blender, combine dressing ingredients; blend. Toss salad lightly with dressing.
12 servings

Mediterranean Salad

Nutritious and colorful.

250	mL	Eston Lentils	1 cup
500	mL	water	2 cups
2		beef bouillon cubes	2
42	g	pkg. dried tomatoes	1½ oz.
2		medium potatoes, peeled, cubed, cooked	2
0.5		onion, chopped	½
125	mL	thinly sliced celery	½ cup
125	mL	chopped cucumber	½ cup
398	mL	can baby corn, drained, chopped	14 oz.
1		large carrot, grated	1
125	mL	sliced mushrooms	½ cup
250	mL	grated low-fat Cheddar cheese	1 cup

Lemon Dill Dressing:

45	mL	lemon juice	3 tbsp.
125	mL	canola oil	½ cup
5	mL	Mrs. Dash extra spicy seasoning	1 tsp.
5	mL	celery salt	1 tsp.
2		garlic cloves, minced	2
10	mL	finely chopped fresh dillweed	2 tsp.
		pita pockets OR lettuce	

- Rinse and drain lentils. In a saucepan, combine lentils, water and bouillon. Bring to a boil, cover, reduce heat and simmer 30 minutes. Drain and cool.
- Cover dried tomatoes with boiling water; let stand 2 minutes. Drain and slice into slivers.
- Combine lentils, vegetables and cheese.
- In a blender, combine lemon juice, oil, and seasonings, blend. Drizzle dressing over salad and toss again.
- Serve in a pita pocket or on a lettuce bed.
  12 servings

Yield:	1.5 L (6 cups)
Serving Size:	125 mL (½ cup)
Preparation Time:	45 minutes
Pulse Product:	Eston Lentils

Nutritional Analysis (per serving)

Calories:	208	
Total Fat:	13	g
Saturated Fat:	3	g
Protein:	7.5	g
Carbohydrates:	17	g
Cholesterol:	10	mg
Sodium:	393	mg
Potassium:	368	mg
Folic Acid:	8	mcg
Total Fiber:	2	g
Soluble:	0.5	g
Insoluble:	1.5	g

Diabetic Food Choices

Protein:	1
Fruit & Vegetables:	1½
Fats & Oils:	2

Pictured on page 71.

Gluten-Free

Yield: 1 L
(4 cups)

Serving Size: 125 mL
(½ cup)

Preparation Time: 30 minutes

Pulse Product: Laird Lentils

Nutritional Analysis
(per serving)

Calories: 179

Total Fat: 15.5 g

Saturated Fat: 1 g

Protein: 2.5 g

Carbohydrates: 9.5 g

Cholesterol: 15 mg

Sodium: 368 mg

Potassium: 197 mg

Folic Acid: 28 mcg

Total Fiber: 3 g

Soluble: 1 g

Insoluble: 2 g

Diabetic Food Choices

Starch: ½

Fats & Oils: 3

Zesty Italiano Salad

The marinating time allows the flavors to blend and mature.

175 mL	Zesty Italian dressing*	¾	cup
250 mL	cooked Laird Lentils, still hot	1	cup
125 mL	sliced carrot	½	cup
125 mL	diced red onion	½	cup
125 mL	sliced celery	½	cup
125 mL	chopped cauliflower	½	cup
125 mL	diced sweet green pepper	½	cup
125 mL	diced sweet yellow pepper	½	cup
	garlic salt to taste		

- Pour Italian dressing over hot lentils and let cool.
- Add carrot, onion, celery, cauliflower, peppers and garlic salt.
- Refrigerate. Let marinate for 24 hours.
8 servings

*Gluten-free brand required

Marinated Bean and Pepperoni Salad

An easy salad to take to a picnic or pot luck supper.

500	mL	cooked Great Northern Beans	2	cups
500	mL	cooked Pink Beans	2	cups
175	mL	diced sweet green pepper	¾	cup
175	mL	sliced celery	¾	cup
125	mL	thinly sliced red onion	½	cup
25	mL	chopped fresh parsley	2	tbsp.

Mediterranean Dressing:

50	mL	canola oil	¼	cup
50	mL	red wine vinegar	¼	cup
7	mL	granulated sugar	1½	tsp.
2	mL	salt	½	tsp.
2	mL	garlic powder	½	tsp.
2	mL	dry mustard	½	tsp.
2	mL	dry crumbled oregano	½	tsp.
2	mL	dry crumbled basil	½	tsp.
125	mL	black olives, thinly sliced	½	cup
375	mL	thinly sliced pepperoni stick*	1½	cups
		green pepper rings		

- In a bowl, mix beans, pepper, celery, onion and parsley.
- In another bowl, combine oil, vinegar, sugar, salt, garlic powder, dry mustard, oregano and basil. Pour over beans, toss. Cover and refrigerate several hours.
- At serving time, toss in black olives and pepperoni. Garnish with green pepper rings.

16 servings

*Gluten-free brand required

Gluten-Free

Yield:	2 L (8 cups)
Serving Size:	125 mL (½ cup)
Preparation Time:	20 minutes
Pulse Product:	Great Northern Beans, Pink Beans

Nutritional Analysis (per serving)

Calories:	410	
Total Fat:	31	g
Saturated Fat:	8	g
Protein:	14.5	g
Carbohydrates:	19	g
Cholesterol:	33	mg
Sodium:	2013	mg
Potassium:	482	mg
Folic Acid:	54	mcg
Total Fiber:	7.5	g
Soluble:	3	g
Insoluble:	4.5	g

Diabetic Food Choices

Protein:	2
Fruit & Vegetables:	1½
Fats & Oils:	5

Yield:	1.25 L (5 cups)
Serving Size:	250 mL (1 cup)
Preparation Time:	30 minutes
Pulse Product:	Pinto Beans

Nutritional Analysis
(per serving)

Calories:	269	
Total Fat:	13.5	g
Saturated Fat:	1	g
Protein:	7.5	g
Carbohydrates:	33.5	g
Cholesterol:	14.5	mg
Sodium:	257	mg
Potassium:	549.5	mg
Folic Acid:	109.5	mcg
Total Fiber:	6.5	g
Soluble:	3	g
Insoluble:	3.5	g

Diabetic Food Choices

Protein:	½
Starch:	1
Fruit & Vegetables:	1
Fats & Oils:	2½

Pictured on page 123.

Mexican Salad Bowl

An easy-to-prepare summertime salad.

500	**mL**	**cooked Pinto Beans**	**2 cups**
125	**mL**	**diced low-fat sharp Cheddar cheese**	**½ cup**
341	**mL**	**can kernel corn, drained**	**12 oz.**
2		**tomatoes, diced**	**2**
125	**mL**	**chopped sweet green pepper**	**½ cup**
125	**mL**	**chopped sweet red pepper**	**½ cup**
2		**green onions, thinly sliced**	**2**
125	**mL**	**calorie-wise French salad dressing**	**½ cup**
2	**mL**	**chili powder**	**½ tsp.**
1		**head iceberg lettuce, shredded**	**1**

- In a bowl, combine beans, cheese, corn, tomato, peppers and onion. Toss lightly.
- Combine dressing and chili powder, pour over salad mixture and toss.
- Cover and refrigerate 1 hour. Serve over shredded lettuce.

5 servings

Mexican Salad

This salad has eye appeal as well as taste appeal.

375	mL	Red Mexican Beans, soaked overnight	1½	cups
375	mL	Eston Lentils	1½	cups
1.5	L	water	6	cups
250	mL	diced tomato	1	cup
75	mL	chopped sweet green pepper	⅓	cup
50	mL	chopped green onion	¼	cup
250	mL	calorie-wise Catalina dressing*	1	cup
500	mL	shredded lettuce	2	cups
250	mL	grated low-fat mozzarella cheese	1	cup

- Drain beans. Combine beans, lentils and water in a large saucepan or Dutch oven. Bring to a boil. Cover, reduce heat and simmer until just tender, about 1 hour. Remove from heat, drain and cool.
- In a bowl, combine beans, lentils, tomato, green pepper and onion. Mix gently.
- Pour dressing over pulse mixture. Cover and refrigerate 12 hours. Mix occasionally.
- Just before serving, place pulse mixture in a wide, shallow serving dish. Top with lettuce and cheese. Serve with tortilla chips.

18 servings

*Gluten-free brand required

Gluten-Free

Yield:	2.5 L (9 cups)
Serving Size:	125 mL (½ cup)
Preparation Time:	20 minutes
Pulse Product:	Eston Lentils Red Mexican Beans

Nutritional Analysis (per serving)

Calories:	147	
Total Fat:	3	g
Saturated Fat:	1	g
Protein:	9	g
Carbohydrates:	22	g
Cholesterol:	4.5	mg
Sodium:	296.5	mg
Potassium:	382	mg
Folic Acid:	71	mcg
Total Fiber:	4.5	g
Soluble:	1.5	g
Insoluble:	3	g

Diabetic Food Choices

Protein:	1
Starch:	1

Gluten-Free

Yield:	1.75 L
	(7 cups)
Serving Size:	125 mL
	(½ cup)
Preparation Time:	35 minutes
Pulse Product:	Eston Lentils

Nutritional Analysis
(per serving)

Calories:	280	
Total Fat:	14.5	g
Saturated Fat:	1.5	g
Protein:	12	g
Carbohydrates:	28	g
Cholesterol:	1	mg
Sodium:	1418	mg
Potassium:	448	mg
Folic Acid:	12	mcg
Total Fiber:	4.5	g
Soluble:	1	g
Insoluble:	3.5	g

Diabetic Food Choices

Protein:	1½
Starch:	1
Fruit & Vegetables:	1
Fats & Oils:	2

Southwest Lentils

A taste sensation from southwest of here.

1.5	L	chicken stock*	6 cups
625	mL	Eston Lentils, rinsed and drained	2½ cups
3		medium carrots, quartered	3
1		medium onion	1
4		whole cloves	4
1		bay leaf	1
10	mL	dry crumbled basil	2 tsp.
125	mL	white vinegar	½ cup
125	mL	canola oil	½ cup
2	mL	dry crushed chilies	½ tsp.
4		garlic cloves, minced	4
2	mL	salt	½ tsp.
2	mL	ground black pepper	½ tsp.
250	mL	sliced green onion	1 cup
250	mL	pine nuts	1 cup
175	mL	chopped sweet green and red peppers	¾ cup
		chopped fresh parsley	

- In a Dutch oven, combine chicken stock, lentils, carrot, onion with cloves stuck in, bay leaf and basil. Bring mixture to a boil. Reduce heat, cover and simmer 30 minutes, or until lentils are just tender.
- In a food processor, purée vinegar, oil, chilies and garlic to make a dressing.
- When lentils are tender, drain and discard carrot, onion, cloves and bay leaf.
- While lentils are still hot, toss gently with dressing. Add salt and pepper. Cool to room temperature, mix again, cover; refrigerate.
- Just before serving, add green onion, pine nuts and sweet peppers. Garnish with parsley.

14 servings

*Gluten-free brand required

Pink Bean & Sauerkraut Slaw

Pink beans make this more than just ordinary sauerkraut slaw.

375	mL	cooked Pink Beans	1½ cups
250	mL	drained sauerkraut	1 cup
125	mL	diced celery	½ cup
125	mL	chopped sweet orange pepper	½ cup
75	mL	low-fat sour cream*	⅓ cup
125	mL	chopped onion	½ cup
25	mL	granulated sugar	2 tbsp.
2	mL	celery seed	½ tsp.
1	mL	dry mustard	¼ tsp.

- In a large bowl, combine beans, sauerkraut, celery, pepper, sour cream, onion, sugar, celery seed and mustard.
- Cover and refrigerate 24 hours before serving, stirring occasionally.

8 servings

*Gluten-free brand required

Gluten-Free

Yield:	1 L (4 cups)
Serving Size:	125 mL (½ cup)
Preparation Time:	20 minutes
Pulse Product:	Pink Beans

Nutritional Analysis
(per serving)

Calories:	47	
Total Fat:	1	g
Saturated Fat:	0.5	g
Protein:	1.5	g
Carbohydrates:	8.5	g
Cholesterol:	3	mg
Sodium:	197	mg
Potassium:	147	mg
Folic Acid:	16	mcg
Total Fiber:	2	g
Soluble:	1	g
Insoluble:	1	g

Diabetic Food Choices

Starch:	½

SIDE DISHES

Gluten-Free

Yield:	3 L (12 cups)
Serving Size:	250 mL (1 cup)
Preparation Time:	30 minutes
Pulse Product:	Pinto Beans

Nutritional Analysis (per serving)

Calories:	301	
Total Fat:	9.5	g
Saturated Fat:	2	g
Protein:	12.5	g
Carbohydrates:	43.5	g
Cholesterol:	21	mg
Sodium:	681.5	mg
Potassium:	868	mg
Folic Acid:	106	mcg
Total Fiber:	8	g
Soluble:	3.5	g
Insoluble:	4.5	g

Diabetic Food Choices

Protein:	½
Starch:	2
Sugar:	1
Fats & Oils:	1½

Can't Beat Baked Beans

You can't beat baked beans — anytime!

750	mL	Pinto Beans, soaked overnight	3 cups
796	mL	can tomatoes	28 oz.
50	mL	margarine	¼ cup
398	mL	pineapple chunks, drained	14 oz.
125	mL	finely chopped celery	½ cup
50	mL	molasses	¼ cup
50	mL	brown sugar	¼ cup
7	mL	salt	1½ tsp.
2	mL	ground black pepper	½ tsp.
500	mL	grated low-fat Cheddar cheese	2 cups

- Drain beans. Place in a large saucepan or Dutch oven and add fresh water to cover. Bring to a boil. Reduce heat, cover and simmer 1 hour, or until beans are tender. Drain.
- Add tomatoes and margarine. Heat until margarine is melted.
- Preheat oven to 180°C (350°F).
- In a bowl, combine pineapple, celery, molasses, brown sugar, salt and pepper. Stir well.
- Place beans in 3 L (3-quart) casserole. Cover with sauce. Top with cheese.
- Cover and bake 1½-2 hours.

12 servings

Ev's Baked Beans

This is a wonderful recipe for barbecues, family get togethers or harvest time. It turns out well in the slow cooker too! Cook on low 10 to 12 hours or high for 4 to 6 hours.

750	mL	Great Northern Beans, soaked overnight	3	cups
2.25	L	water	9	cups
1		onion, chopped	1	
250	mL	ketchup*	1	cup
250	mL	brown sugar	1	cup
250	mL	water	1	cup
10	mL	molasses	2	tsp.
5	mL	seasoned salt	1	tsp.
250	mL	chopped ham*	1	cup

- Drain beans. In a large saucepan or Dutch oven, combine beans and water. Bring to a boil, reduce heat, cover and simmer 30 minutes. Remove from heat and let stand 1½ hours. Drain.
- Preheat oven to 150°C (300°F).
- Place beans in a 4 L (4-quart) casserole. Add onion, ketchup, brown sugar, water, molasses, salt and ham. Stir well.
- Bake, covered, 5-6 hours. Stir occasionally and add water if mixture becomes too dry.

16 servings

*Gluten-free brand required

Gluten-Free

Yield:	2 L (8 cups)
Serving Size:	125 mL (½ cup)
Preparation Time:	25 minutes
Pulse Product:	Great Northern Beans

Nutritional Analysis (per serving)

Calories:	206	
Total Fat:	2	g
Saturated Fat:	0.5	g
Protein:	10	g
Carbohydrates:	39	g
Cholesterol:	4	mg
Sodium:	406.5	mg
Potassium:	612.5	mg
Folic Acid:	70	mcg
Total Fiber:	2.5	g
Soluble:	1	g
Insoluble:	1.5	g

Diabetic Food Choices

Protein:	½
Starch:	2
Sugar:	½

Yield:	1.5 L (6 cups)
Serving Size:	125 mL (½ cup)
Preparation Time:	30 minutes
Pulse Product:	Great Northern Beans

Nutritional Analysis
(per serving)

Calories:	216	
Total Fat:	11	g
Saturated Fat:	5	g
Protein:	9	g
Carbohydrates:	20.5	g
Cholesterol:	12.5	mg
Sodium:	242.5	mg
Potassium:	500	mg
Folic Acid:	64	mcg
Total Fiber:	2.5	g
Soluble:	1	g
Insoluble:	1.5	g

Diabetic Food Choices

Protein:	1
Starch:	1
Fats & Oils:	1½

More Beans Please

Serve with pumpernickel bread after a day on the ski trails.*

500	**mL**	**Great Northern Beans, soaked overnight**	**2**	**cups**
1.5	**L**	**water**	**6**	**cups**
1		**large Spanish onion, chopped**	**1**	
3		**sprigs of fresh parsley**	**3**	
227	**g**	**sliced bacon****	**½**	**lb.**
213	**mL**	**can tomato sauce****	**7½**	**oz.**
2	**mL**	**salt**	**½**	**tsp.**
1	**mL**	**ground black pepper**	**¼**	**tsp.**

- Drain beans. In a large saucepan, combine beans, water, onion, parsley and bacon. Bring to a boil over medium heat. Reduce heat, cover and simmer 1 hour and 15 minutes, or until beans are firm-tender.
- Drain beans and onion. Discard parsley and remove bacon.
- Dice bacon and brown in a small skillet over medium heat.
- Add tomato sauce, salt and pepper to beans, return to low heat, cover and simmer 10 minutes.
- Add bacon and simmer 5 minutes longer. Serve hot.

12 servings

*Not gluten-free
**Gluten-free brand required

Country Beans

Country beans for a banquet or family supper! Use rubber gloves when dicing red chili peppers.

1.25	L	cooked Pinto Beans	5	cups
375	mL	peeled, chopped tomato	1½	cups
125	mL	chopped celery	½	cup
125	mL	chopped onion	½	cup
50	mL	chopped sweet green pepper	¼	cup
50	mL	tomato paste	¼	cup
25	mL	lemon juice	2	tbsp.
15	mL	canola oil	1	tbsp.
2	mL	cumin	½	tsp.
2		garlic cloves, minced	2	
2	mL	finely diced hot red chili pepper	½	tsp.
2		dashes Tabasco sauce	2	
5	mL	salt (optional)	1	tsp.
1	mL	ground black pepper (optional)	¼	tsp.

- Place beans in a large saucepan or Dutch oven.
- Add tomato, celery, onion, green pepper, tomato paste, lemon juice, oil, cumin, garlic, chili pepper and Tabasco sauce.
- Cover and simmer, stirring frequently, until celery and onion are tender. If necessary add a little liquid to prevent scorching.
- Prior to serving add salt and pepper if desired.

8 servings

Gluten-Free

Yield:	2 L (8 cups)
Serving Size:	250 mL (1 cup)
Preparation Time:	30 minutes
Pulse Product:	Pinto Beans

Nutritional Analysis (per serving)

Calories:	90	
Total Fat:	2.5	g
Saturated Fat:	trace	
Protein:	3.5	g
Carbohydrates:	15	g
Cholesterol:	0	mg
Sodium:	348.5	mg
Potassium:	341.5	mg
Folic Acid:	30	mcg
Total Fiber:	11	g
Soluble:	5	g
Insoluble:	6	g

Diabetic Food Choices

Starch:	1
Fats & Oils:	1

Three Bean Bake

A great dish to take to pot luck suppers!

398	mL	can Baked Beans	14	oz.
398	mL	can Lima Beans	14	oz.
398	mL	can Kidney Beans	14	oz.
500	mL	chopped onion	2	cups
250	mL	chopped sweet green pepper	1	cup
2		garlic cloves, minced	2	
25	mL	canola oil	2	tbsp.
15	mL	all-purpose flour	1	tbsp.
25	mL	molasses	2	tbsp.
15	mL	sodium-reduced soy sauce	1	tbsp.
2	mL	ground ginger	½	tsp.
		pinch of chili powder		

- Preheat oven to 160°C (325°F).
- Combine Baked, Lima and Kidney Beans in a 2 L (2-quart) casserole.
- In a large skillet, sauté onion, pepper and garlic in oil until onion is translucent.
- Stir in flour then add molasses, soy sauce, ginger and chili powder. Bring to a boil. Pour over beans and stir lightly.
- Cover and bake 1 hour. Uncover and bake 30 minutes, or until thick.

6 servings

Yield:	1.5 L (6 cups)
Serving Size:	250 mL (1 cup)
Preparation Time:	15 minutes
Pulse Product:	Kidney Beans Navy Beans Lima Beans

Nutritional Analysis (per serving)

Calories:	266	
Total Fat:	7	g
Saturated Fat:	1	g
Protein:	11.5	g
Carbohydrates:	40.5	g
Cholesterol:	3	mg
Sodium:	211.5	mg
Potassium:	652	mg
Folic Acid:	30	mcg
Total Fiber:	10	g
Soluble:	5	g
Insoluble:	5	g

Diabetic Food Choices

Protein:	1
Starch:	2
Fats & Oils:	1

Refried Beans

A classic Mexican dish to serve with chicken or fish. You can replace Red Mexican Beans with any leftover cooked beans.

500	**mL**	**cooked Red Mexican Beans**	**2**	**cups**
2		**slices bacon**	**2**	
50	**mL**	**chopped onion**	**¼**	**cup**
		dash of hot red pepper sauce		
1	**mL**	**chili powder**	**¼**	**tsp.**
1	**mL**	**salt**	**¼**	**tsp.**
1		**garlic clove, minced**	**1**	
15-25	**mL**	**canola oil**	**1-2**	**tbsp.**

- Mash beans thoroughly.
- In a small saucepan, cook bacon until crisp. Drain on paper towel and crumble.
- In bacon fat, sauté onion until soft. Cool slightly. Drain off excess fat.
- In a bowl, combine beans, bacon, onion, pepper sauce, chili powder, salt and garlic; mix thoroughly.
- Add just enough oil to make the bean mixture smooth.

8 servings

Yield:	500 mL (2 cups)
Serving Size:	50 mL (¼ cup)
Preparation Time:	15 minutes
Pulse Product:	Red Mexican Beans

Nutritional Analysis (per serving)

Calories:	75	
Total Fat:	4	g
Saturated Fat:	0.5	g
Protein:	3	g
Carbohydrates:	7.5	g
Cholesterol:	2	mg
Sodium:	93	mg
Potassium:	131	mg
Folic Acid:	10.5	mcg
Total Fiber:	3	g
Soluble:	1.5	g
Insoluble:	1.5	g

Diabetic Food Choices

Protein:	½
Starch:	½
Fats & Oils:	½

Yield:	1 L
	(4 cups)
Serving Size:	125 mL
	(½ cup)
Preparation Time:	15 minutes
Pulse Product:	Rose Lentils

Nutritional Analysis
(per serving)

Calories:	284	
Total Fat:	7.5	g
Saturated Fat:	4.5	g
Protein:	8.5	g
Carbohydrates:	46.5	g
Cholesterol:	0	mg
Sodium:	235	mg
Potassium:	317	mg
Folic Acid:	12.5	mcg
Total Fiber:	3	g
Soluble:	0.5	g
Insoluble:	2.5	g

Diabetic Food Choices

Protein:	½
Starch:	2½
Fats & Oils:	1

Rose Lentils and Rice

A *delicious, very easy dish to prepare.*

125	mL	Rose Lentils	½	cup
250	mL	brown rice	1	cup
175	mL	coconut milk	¾	cup
550	mL	water	2¼	cups
1		small onion, chopped	1	
15	mL	margarine	1	tbsp.
1	mL	dry crumbled thyme	¼	tsp.
1	mL	garlic powder	¼	tsp.
2	mL	curry powder	½	tsp.
1	mL	ground ginger	¼	tsp.
2	mL	salt	½	tsp.

- In a saucepan, combine lentils, rice, coconut milk, water, onion, margarine, thyme, garlic powder, curry, ginger and salt. Stir.
- Bring to a boil, cover and simmer 50 minutes.

8 servings

Multi-Grain Pilaf

This tasty dish is easy to assemble.

1	medium onion, chopped	1	
15 mL	canola oil	1	tbsp.
125 mL	Eston Lentils	½	cup
125 mL	sliced almonds	½	cup
125 mL	wild rice	½	cup
125 mL	brown rice	½	cup
125 mL	pot barley	½	cup
2	chicken bouillon cubes	2	
1.125 L	hot water	4½	cups
5 mL	Mrs. Dash table blend seasoning*	1	tsp.
25 mL	cooking sherry	2	tbsp.

- Preheat oven to 180°C (350°F).
- Sauté onion in oil until onion is translucent.
- Add lentils, almonds, wild rice, brown rice and barley. Stir until slightly browned.
- Dissolve chicken bouillon cubes in hot water and add to lentil mixture.
- Add Mrs. Dash seasoning and sherry.
- Pour into a 2 L (2-quart) casserole. Cover and bake 1¼ hours.

12 servings

* Mrs. Dash is a salt-free blend of herbs and spices. Substitute seasoned pepper and/or dried crumbled oregano, thyme, parsley, basil, savory, etc., to your taste.

Yield:	1.5 L (6 cups)
Serving Size:	125 mL (½ cup)
Preparation Time:	10 minutes
Pulse Product:	Eston Lentils

Nutritional Analysis (per serving)

Calories:	172	
Total Fat:	5	g
Saturated Fat:	0.5	g
Protein:	5.5	g
Carbohydrates:	26	g
Cholesterol:	trace	
Sodium:	163	mg
Potassium:	184	mg
Folic Acid:	7	mcg
Total Fiber:	2.5	g
Soluble:	0.5	g
Insoluble:	2	g

Diabetic Food Choices

Protein:	½
Starch:	1½
Fats & Oils:	½

Gluten-Free

Yield:	750 mL (3 cups)
Serving Size:	125 mL (½ cup)
Preparation Time:	15 minutes
Pulse Product:	Eston Lentils

Nutritional Analysis
(per serving)

Calories:	173	
Total Fat:	5	g
Saturated Fat:	0.5	g
Protein:	9	g
Carbohydrates:	24	g
Cholesterol:	trace	
Sodium:	308	mg
Potassium:	358.5	mg
Folic Acid:	10.5	mcg
Total Fiber:	3.5	g
Soluble:	1	g
Insoluble:	2.5	g

Diabetic Food Choices

Protein:	1
Starch:	1
Fats & Oils:	½

Lentil Pilaf

An easy addition to any meal.

250	mL	chopped onion	1	cup
25	mL	finely chopped fresh dillweed	2	tbsp.
25	mL	canola oil	2	tbsp.
250	mL	Eston Lentils	1	cup
284	mL	can sliced mushrooms, drained	10	oz.
500	mL	boiling water	2	cups
15	mL	light chicken bouillon powder*	1	tbsp.

- In a large saucepan or Dutch oven, sauté onion and dill in oil until onion is translucent.
- Add lentils and mushrooms. Cook 5 minutes.
- Add water and chicken bouillon powder. Cover and simmer 40-50 minutes, or until lentils are tender.

6 servings

*Gluten-free brand required

Spicy Hot Split Peas

"Pease porridge," of nursery rhyme fame, was made from dried Yellow Split Peas, served hot or cold or even nine days old!

500	mL	Yellow Split Peas	2	cups
50	mL	sodium-reduced soy sauce*	¼	cup
90	mL	honey	6	tbsp.
10	mL	minced ginger root	2	tsp.
10	mL	cornstarch	2	tsp.
25	mL	water	2	tbsp.
15	mL	sesame oil	1	tbsp.
10		garlic cloves, minced	10	
5	mL	dry crumbled red chili pepper	1	tsp.
125	mL	diced sweet red pepper	½	cup
125	mL	currants	½	cup
		cooked white rice		

- Rinse peas; cover with water; bring to a boil; cover, reduce heat and simmer 30 minutes. Drain.
- In a small bowl, combine soy sauce, honey, ginger, cornstarch and water. Set aside.
- In a saucepan, heat oil, garlic and chili pepper. Do not brown. Add peas, sweet pepper and currants. Sauté 5 minutes, stirring constantly.
- Add soy mixture and cook, stirring constantly, until mixture is thickened, clear and heated through.
- Serve on a bed of rice.

6 servings

*Gluten-free brand required

Gluten-Free

Yield:	1.5 L (6 cups)
Serving Size:	250 mL (1 cup)
Preparation Time:	25 minutes
Pulse Product:	Yellow Split Peas

Nutritional Analysis (per serving)

Calories:	235	
Total Fat:	3	g
Saturated Fat:	0.5	g
Protein:	8.5	g
Carbohydrates:	48	g
Cholesterol:	0	mg
Sodium:	582.5	mg
Potassium:	431	mg
Folic Acid:	7	mcg
Total Fiber:	2	g
Soluble:	1	g
Insoluble:	1	g

Diabetic Food Choices

Protein:	½
Starch:	2
Fruit & Vegetables:	1

Chickpeas & Apricots

Chickpeas with a difference!

Yield:	1 L (4 cups)
Serving Size:	250 mL (1 cup)
Preparation Time:	20 minutes
Pulse Product:	Chickpeas

Nutritional Analysis (per serving)

Calories:	220	
Total Fat:	6	g
Saturated Fat:	0.5	g
Protein:	9.5	g
Carbohydrates:	34.5	g
Cholesterol:	5	mg
Sodium:	1155	mg
Potassium:	646	mg
Folic Acid:	80	mcg
Total Fiber:	9	g
Soluble:	4	g
Insoluble:	5	g

Diabetic Food Choices

Protein:	1
Starch:	½
Sugar:	½
Fruits & Vegetables:	1½
Fats & Oils:	½

15	mL	canola oil	1 tbsp.
250	mL	chopped onion	1 cup
540	mL	can Chickpeas, rinsed and drained	19 oz.
4		garlic cloves, minced	4
540	mL	can Mexican spiced stewed tomatoes	19 oz.
5	mL	dry crumbled oregano	1 tsp.
2	mL	salt	½ tsp.
2	mL	ground black pepper	½ tsp.
2	mL	cumin	½ tsp.
175	mL	chopped dried apricots	¾ cup
125	mL	water	½ cup

- In a large saucepan, heat oil and sauté onion until soft.
- Add Chickpeas, garlic, tomatoes, oregano, salt, pepper, cumin and apricots. Stir together and sauté 5 minutes.
- Add water. Simmer, covered, 30-45 minutes, or until apricots are tender.
- Add more water if required.

4 servings

Couscous with Autumn Vegetables

Cook this tasty medley in the late summer, when garden vegetables are at their best.

15	mL	canola oil	1	tbsp.
1		garlic clove, minced	1	
125	mL	diced onion	½	cup
2	mL	cinnamon	½	tsp.
2	mL	turmeric	½	tsp.
2	mL	paprika	½	tsp.
2	mL	cumin	½	tsp.
1	mL	cayenne pepper	¼	tsp.
625	mL	chicken broth*	2½	cups
250	mL	diced carrot	1	cup
250	mL	diced turnip	1	cup
375	mL	cooked Chickpeas OR 398 mL (14 oz.) can Chickpeas, rinsed, drained	1½	cups
175	mL	chopped sweet red pepper	¾	cup
125	mL	diced green OR yellow zucchini	½	cup
250	mL	couscous	1	cup
25	mL	chopped fresh parsley	2	tbsp.

- In a large saucepan, heat oil. Add garlic and onion. Sauté until onion is translucent.
- Add cinnamon, turmeric, paprika, cumin and cayenne pepper. Stir.
- Add broth, carrot and turnip. Cover; simmer 10-15 minutes, or until vegetables are tender.
- Add Chickpeas, sweet pepper and zucchini, and simmer 5 minutes.
- Add couscous. Turn off heat and let stand 5 minutes, or until liquid is absorbed.
- Garnish with parsley.

7 servings

*Gluten-free brand required

Gluten-Free

Yield:	1.75 L (7 cups)
Serving Size:	250 mL (1 cup)
Preparation Time:	45 minutes
Pulse Product:	Chickpeas

Nutritional Analysis (per serving)

Calories:	172	
Total Fat:	7	g
Saturated Fat:	trace	
Protein:	8	g
Carbohydrates:	20.5	g
Cholesterol:	3	mg
Sodium:	88	mg
Potassium:	350.5	mg
Folic Acid:	38.5	mcg
Total Fiber:	5.5	g
Soluble:	2.5	g
Insoluble:	3	g

Diabetic Food Choices

Protein:	1
Fruit & Vegetables:	1½
Fats & Oils:	1

Pictured on cover.

Yield:	12 pieces
Serving Size:	1 piece
Preparation Time:	40 minutes
Pulse Product:	Great Northern Beans

Nutritional Analysis
(per serving)

Calories:	369	
Total Fat:	22	g
Saturated Fat:	7	g
Protein:	14	g
Carbohydrates:	28.5	g
Cholesterol:	54.5	mg
Sodium:	802	mg
Potassium:	390	mg
Folic Acid:	31	mcg
Total Fiber:	3	g
Soluble:	1.5	g
Insoluble:	1.5	g

Diabetic Food Choices

Protein:	1½
Starch:	1
Fruit & Vegetables:	1
Fats & Oils:	3½

Lazy Pyroghy

Lazy pyroghies, but not lazy on taste!

9		lasagne noodles, cooked	9	
375	mL	mashed potatoes	1½	cups
375	mL	Great Northern Bean purée	1½	cups
250	mL	grated low-fat Cheddar cheese	1	cup
500	mL	low-fat creamed cottage cheese	2	cups
50	mL	thinly sliced green onion	¼	cup
1		egg, slightly beaten	1	
5	mL	salt	1	tsp.
2	mL	ground black pepper	½	tsp.
300	g	pkg. frozen spinach, thawed	10	oz.
375	mL	diced onion	1½	cups
50	mL	margarine	¼	cup
227	g	bacon, cooked crisp and crumbled	½	lb.

- Preheat oven to 180°C (350°F).
- Spray a 22 x 34 cm (9 x 13") baking dish with a nonstick vegetable spray.
- Place 3 lasagne noodles on the pan bottom.
- In a bowl, combine potatoes, bean purée and Cheddar cheese. Spread over noodles. Cover with 3 more lasagne noodles.
- Combine cottage cheese, onion, egg, salt and pepper. Add drained spinach. Mix well. Spread over second layer of noodles. Cover with remaining noodles.
- In a skillet, sauté onion in margarine until translucent. Remove from heat. Spread over final layer of noodles.
- Cover with foil and bake 1¼ hours.
- Remove pyroghy from oven. Garnish with bacon and bake, uncovered, for 5 minutes.
- Let stand 10 minutes, covered, before serving. Cut into 12 pieces.

12 servings.

Lentil-Stuffed Zucchini

Sweet green peppers and tomatoes may also be stuffed. Use 3 sweet green peppers baked at 200°C (400°F), 40-45 minutes or 4 tomatoes baked at 180°C (350°F), 30-40 minutes.

2		medium zucchini	2
175	mL	cooked Eston Lentils	¾ cup
50	mL	Minute Rice (uncooked)	¼ cup
25	mL	finely chopped onion	2 tbsp.
5	mL	canola oil	1 tsp.
25	mL	tomato paste	2 tbsp.
1	mL	dry crumbled mint	¼ tsp.
		salt and ground black pepper to taste	
125	mL	water	½ cup
25	mL	lemon juice	2 tbsp.

- Preheat oven to 200°C (400°F).
- Cut ends off zucchini, slice in half lengthwise, remove center seed area.
- Combine lentils, rice, onion, oil, tomato paste, mint, salt and pepper. Mix thoroughly.
- Stuff zucchini with lentil mixture. Arrange in a 22 x 34 cm (9 x 13") baking pan; add water to pan; sprinkle with lemon juice. Loosely cover pan with foil.
- Bake 45-50 minutes. Serve with Zesty Lemon Hollandaise Sauce (see next page). To serve, cut each stuffed half zucchini into half again.

8 servings

Gluten-Free

Yield:	300 mL (1¼ cups)
Serving Size:	¼ zucchini stuffed with 45 mL (3 tbsp.) filling
Preparation Time:	30 minutes
Pulse Product:	Eston Lentils

Nutritional Analysis (per serving)

Calories:	75	
Total Fat:	2.5	g
Saturated Fat:	1	g
Protein:	5	g
Carbohydrates:	10	g
Cholesterol:	69	mg
Sodium:	231	mg
Potassium:	250	mg
Folic Acid:	16	mcg
Total Fiber:	1	g
Soluble:	trace	
Insoluble:	1	g

Diabetic Food Choices

Protein:	½
Starch:	½

Pictured on page 105.

Yield: 250 mL
                (1 cup)

Serving Size: 50 mL
                (¼ cup)
                per half stuffed
                zucchini

Preparation Time: 25 minutes

Zesty Lemon Hollandaise

Sauce may be made in advance and reheated over hot, not simmering, water. May be refrigerated for up to 1 week.

250	mL	low-fat plain yogurt*	1 cup
10	mL	lemon juice	2 tsp.
1	mL	grated lemon rind	¼ tsp.
2		egg yolks	2
1		garlic clove, minced	1
2	mL	salt	½ tsp.
		pinch of ground black pepper	
5	mL	Dijon mustard	1 tsp.
15	mL	dry crumbled dillweed	1 tbsp.

- In a bowl, beat together yogurt, lemon juice, lemon rind, yolks and garlic.
- Pour into a saucepan and heat over medium-low heat, 15 minutes or until sauce has thickened, stirring frequently. Remove from heat.
- Add salt, pepper, mustard and dill. Stir well. Serve over Lentil-Stuffed Zucchini.

*Gluten-free brand required

Texans

Pulses can even be used in cabbage rolls!
Use rubber gloves with jalapeños.

1	medium head cabbage	1
1	medium onion, diced	1
1	large sweet green pepper, diced	1
1	jalapeño pepper, diced	1
5	garlic cloves, minced	5
5 mL	canola oil	1 tsp.
2	tomatoes, diced	2
25 mL	tomato paste	2 tbsp.
500 mL	cooked Eston Lentils	2 cups
500 mL	cooked rice	2 cups
2 mL	cumin	½ tsp.
10 mL	chili powder	2 tsp.
375 mL	grated low-fat Cheddar cheese	1½ cups
750 mL	tomato juice	3 cups

- With a sharp knife, core cabbage. Steam cabbage head in a Dutch oven of boiling water. Remove outer leaves as they soften and become pliable, about 4 minutes. You need 22 leaves.
- Preheat oven to 180°C (350°F).
- Sauté onion, pepper, jalapeño and garlic in oil over medium-low heat 10 minutes.
- Add tomatoes and tomato paste. Simmer 10 minutes or until juice forms and tomatoes can be easily broken up.
- Add lentils, rice, cumin and chili powder. Stir well, remove from heat. Mix in cheese.
- Place 50 mL (¼ cup) of lentil filling in a cabbage leaf and roll up, tucking in sides.
- Place rolls side by side in a 22 x 34 cm (9 x 13") baking dish. Pour 750 mL (3 cups) tomato juice over, cover and bake 1 hour.

11 servings

Yield:	22 Texans
Serving Size:	2 Texans
Preparation Time:	50 minutes
Pulse Product:	Eston Lentils

Nutritional Analysis
(per serving)

Calories:	51	
Total Fat:	0.5	g
Saturated Fat:	trace	
Protein:	2.5	g
Carbohydrates:	10	g
Cholesterol:	1	mg
Sodium:	115.5	mg
Potassium:	182.5	mg
Folic Acid:	13	mcg
Total Fiber:	3	g
Soluble:	1	g
Insoluble:	2	g

Diabetic Food Choices

Protein:	½
1% Milk	½
Starch:	½
Fruit & Vegetables:	1

Lentil-Stuffed Zucchini, page 102

Yield:	9 pieces
Serving Size:	1 piece
Preparation Time:	30 minutes
Pulse Product:	Pinto Beans

Nutritional Analysis
(per serving)

Calories:	227	
Total Fat:	14	g
Saturated Fat:	6.5	g
Protein:	7	g
Carbohydrates:	18	g
Cholesterol:	14.5	mg
Sodium:	314	mg
Potassium:	114.5	mg
Folic Acid:	17	mcg
Total Fiber:	4	g
Soluble:	2	g
Insoluble:	2	g

Diabetic Food Choices

Protein:	½
Starch:	½
Fruit & Vegetables:	1
Fats & Oils:	2½

Perfect Pinto Puff

A different way to serve beans!

540	g	pkg. pie crust mix OR	19	oz.
		pastry equal to a top and bottom pie crust		

Bean Layer:

250	mL	cooked Pinto Beans	1	cup
15	mL	butter	1	tbsp.
2		garlic cloves, minced	2	

Spinach Cheese Layer:

250	mL	chopped fresh spinach	1	cup
125	mL	low-fat creamed cottage cheese	½	cup
175	mL	grated low-fat mozzarella cheese	¾	cup
1		egg white	1	

- Preheat oven to 180°C (350°F).
- Divide pastry in half. Form 2, 18 x 22 cm (7 x 9") rectangles. Place 1 on a cookie sheet.
- In a bowl, mash beans with butter and garlic. Spread bean mixture on pastry. Layer with spinach, cottage cheese and mozzarella cheese, leaving at least a 2.5 cm (1") edge all around.
- Cover filling with other rectangle of pastry and fold edges to seal. Slash top crust to allow steam to escape. Decorate with pastry leaves or glaze by brushing top with egg white.
- Bake 20 minutes. Reduce heat to 160°C (325°F), bake 10 minutes more. Cut into 9 pieces.

9 servings

Spanakopita

A delicious Greek spinach pie.

15 mL	canola oil	1	tbsp.
125 mL	diced onion	½	cup
50 mL	sliced green onion	¼	cup
300 g	pkg. chopped frozen, spinach, thawed, well drained	10	oz.
25 mL	finely chopped fresh parsley	2	tbsp.
15 mL	finely chopped fresh dillweed	1	tbsp.
5 mL	salt	1	tsp.
2 mL	ground black pepper	½	tsp.
500 mL	cooked Yellow Split Peas (just until tender)	2	cups
50 mL	1% milk	¼	cup
250 mL	crumbled feta cheese	1	cup
2	eggs	2	
8	phyllo pastry sheets	8	
125 mL	margarine, melted	½	cup

- Preheat oven to 180°C (350°F).
- In a skillet, heat oil and sauté onion until translucent. Add green onion; cook until soft. Add spinach, parsley, dill, salt and pepper. Remove from heat. Stir in peas and milk.
- In a bowl, combine cheese and eggs. Add to pea mixture. Mix well.
- Spray a 22 x 34 cm (9 x 13") baking dish with nonstick vegetable spray. Line dish with 6 phyllo sheets, brushing each with margarine. Do not trim over-hanging sheets. Pour in pea mixture. Fold over-hanging phyllo over mixture.
- Top with 2 phyllo sheets; brush each sheet with margarine; fold to fit the pan. Brush top with margarine. Score phyllo pastry into squares or diamond shapes.
- Bake 45 minutes. Let stand 10 minutes before serving. Cut into 12 pieces.
  12 servings

Yield:	12 pieces
Serving Size:	1 piece
Preparation Time:	30 minutes
Pulse Product:	Yellow Split Peas

Nutritional Analysis (per serving)

Calories:	319	
Total Fat:	25	g
Saturated Fat:	7	g
Protein:	10	g
Carbohydrates:	14.5	g
Cholesterol:	57	mg
Sodium:	722	mg
Potassium:	337	mg
Folic Acid:	29	mcg
Total Fiber:	1.5	g
Soluble:	0.5	g
Insoluble:	1	g

Diabetic Food Choices

Protein:	1½
Fruit & Vegetables:	1
Fat & Oils:	4

Yield: 1.5 L (6 cups)

Serving Size: 250 mL (1 cup)

Preparation Time: 20 minutes

Pulse Product: Pinto Beans

Nutritional Analysis (per serving)

Calories:	238	
Total Fat:	6	g
Saturated Fat:	0.5	g
Protein:	9	g
Carbohydrates:	41	g
Cholesterol:	0	g
Sodium:	473.5	mg
Potassium:	677	mg
Folic Acid:	78	mcg
Total Fiber:	8	g
Soluble:	3.5	g
Insoluble:	4.5	g

Diabetic Food Choices

Protein:	½
Starch:	2
Fruit & Vegetables:	½
Fats & Oils:	1

Nancy's Pinto Bean Curry

If you like curried dishes you will love this one. Serve on a bed of rice.

1		medium onion, chopped	1	
25	mL	canola oil	2	tbsp.
1		apple, cored, chopped	1	
3		celery stalks	3	
284	mL	can sliced mushrooms, drained	10	oz.
45	mL	curry powder	3	tbsp.
25	mL	all-purpose flour	2	tbsp.
500	mL	water	2	cups
5	mL	ground black pepper	1	tsp.
5	mL	salt	1	tsp.
15	mL	lemon juice	1	tbsp.
125	mL	raisins	½	cup
25	mL	chutney	2	tbsp.
750	mL	cooked Pinto Beans	3	cups

- In a large saucepan, sauté onions in oil until lightly browned.
- Add apple and celery and cook 3-4 minutes.
- Add mushrooms, curry powder and flour, and cook 2-3 minutes, stirring continuously.
- Slowly add water and stir until thick and smooth.
- Add pepper, salt, lemon juice, raisins, chutney and beans. Cook 5-10 minutes, stirring occasionally.

6 servings

Red Mex Stir-Fry

Kidney beans can be substituted for Red Mexican beans.

125	mL	condensed light chicken broth*	½	cup
15	mL	cooking sherry	1	tbsp.
25	mL	sodium-reduced soy sauce*	2	tbsp.
25	mL	cornstarch	2	tbsp.
15	mL	canola oil	1	tbsp.
1		garlic clove, minced	1	
25	mL	finely chopped ginger root	2	tbsp.
1		large carrot, sliced	1	
250	mL	chopped broccoli	1	cup
500	mL	cooked Red Mexican Beans	2	cups
250	mL	chopped celery	1	cup
125	mL	sliced green onion	½	cup
125	mL	sliced almonds	½	cup

- In a bowl, combine chicken broth, sherry, soy sauce and cornstarch. Mix well and set aside.
- In a large skillet or wok, heat oil over high heat; stir-fry garlic and ginger 1 minute.
- Add carrots and broccoli; stir-fry 2 minutes.
- Add beans, celery and onion; stir-fry 3 minutes, or until vegetables are tender-crisp.
- Add chicken broth sauce and heat until it begins to thicken.
- Remove from heat.
- Sprinkle with almonds before serving.

5 servings

*Gluten-free brand required

Gluten-Free

Yield:	1.25 L (5 cups)
Serving Size:	250 mL (1 cup)
Preparation Time:	25 minutes
Pulse Product:	Red Mexican Beans

Nutritional Analysis (per serving)

Calories:	267	
Total Fat:	12	g
Saturated Fat:	1	g
Protein:	12	g
Carbohydrates:	29	g
Cholesterol:	trace	
Sodium:	83.5	mg
Potassium:	705	mg
Folic Acid:	67	mcg
Total Fiber:	9	g
Soluble:	4	g
Insoluble:	5	g

Diabetic Food Choices

Protein:	1
Starch:	1
Fruit & Vegetables:	1
Fats & Oils:	2

Lent-olé Burrito

Meatless burritos — great for lunch.

375 mL	Eston Lentils, washed and drained	1½	cups
750 mL	water	3	cups
1	medium onion, diced	1	
250 mL	diced sweet green pepper	1	cup
2	large garlic cloves, minced	2	
10 mL	canola oil	2	tsp.
7 mL	chili powder	1½	tsp.
2 mL	cumin	½	tsp.
2 mL	garlic powder	½	tsp.
250 mL	water	1	cup
90 mL	tomato paste	6	tbsp.
6-8	tortillas	6-8	
	low-fat sour cream to taste		
	grated low-fat Cheddar cheese to taste		
	Lentil Salsa (see page 30)		

- In a saucepan, combine lentils and water; bring to a boil. Reduce heat; cover and simmer 30 minutes. Drain off any excess water.
- In a skillet, over medium heat, sauté onion, pepper and garlic in oil 2 minutes.
- Add chili powder, cumin, garlic powder, lentils, water and tomato paste. Stir until it starts to thicken. Cover; cook over medium-low heat 10 minutes. Reduce heat; cook 5 minutes.
- Lay a flour tortilla flat, spoon 75-125 mL (⅓-½ cup) lentil mixture down center of each tortilla. Roll up and serve on a plate of shredded lettuce.
- Top with sour cream, Lentil Salsa and cheese.
- Garnish ideas: chopped onions, green peppers, jalapeño peppers or black olives.

6-8 servings

Yield:	6-8 tortillas
Serving Size:	1 tortilla
Preparation Time:	25 minutes
Pulse Product:	Eston Lentils

Nutritional Analysis
(per serving)

Calories:	133	
Total Fat:	2.5	g
Saturated Fat:	trace	
Protein:	5.5	g
Carbohydrates:	25.5	g
Cholesterol:	0	mg
Sodium:	49	mg
Potassium:	273	mg
Folic Acid:	15.5	mcg
Total Fiber:	4	g
Soluble:	1	g
Insoluble:	3	g

Diabetic Food Choices

Protein:	½
Starch:	1½

Rene's Tamale Pie

Tamale pie — full of beans!

Yield:	2.5 L (10 cups)
Serving Size:	250 mL (1 cup)
Preparation Time:	50 minutes
Pulse Product:	Great Northern Beans

Filling:

1	large onion, chopped	1	
3	garlic cloves, minced	3	
25 mL	canola oil	2	tbsp.
4	medium tomatoes, chopped	4	
1	large sweet green pepper, chopped	1	
213 mL	can tomato sauce	7½	oz.
25 mL	chili powder	2	tbsp.
7 mL	salt	1½	tsp.
250 mL	black olives	1	cup
1 L	cooked Great Northern Beans	4	cups

Crust:

250 mL	cornmeal	1	cup
500 mL	milk	2	cups
15 mL	canola oil	1	tbsp.
5 mL	salt	1	tsp.
2	eggs	2	

- To prepare filling: In a large saucepan, sauté onion and garlic in oil until translucent.
- Add tomatoes, pepper, tomato sauce, chili powder, salt and olives. Heat until just boiling. Reduce heat, cover and simmer 20 minutes. Add beans. Place in 2 L (2-quart) casserole.
- Preheat oven to 180°C (350°F).
- To prepare crust: In a saucepan, combine cornmeal, milk, oil, salt and eggs. Heat over medium heat until thickened, stirring frequently.
- Cover bean mixture with cornmeal mush. Bake 40 minutes, or until crust is light brown.

10 servings

Nutritional Analysis
(per serving)

Calories:	242	
Total Fat:	10	g
Saturated Fat:	1.5	g
Protein:	9	g
Carbohydrates:	31	g
Cholesterol:	57	mg
Sodium:	1147	mg
Potassium:	515	mg
Folic Acid:	29	mcg
Total Fiber:	7	g
Soluble:	3	g
Insoluble:	4	g

Diabetic Food Choices

Protein:	1
Starch:	1
Fruit & Vegetables:	1
Fats & Oils:	1

Yield:	6 slices
Serving Size:	1 slice
Preparation Time:	30 minutes
Pulse Product:	Laird Lentils
	Kidney Beans

Nutritional Analysis
(per serving)

Calories:	305	
Total Fat:	9	g
Saturated Fat:	2	g
Protein:	21	g
Carbohydrates:	40.5	g
Cholesterol:	101.5	mg
Sodium:	1059.5	mg
Potassium:	703	mg
Folic Acid:	49	mcg
Total Fiber:	8.5	g
Soluble:	3	g
Insoluble:	5.5	g

Diabetic Food Choices

Protein:	2
Starch:	2
Fruit & Vegetables:	½
Fats & Oils:	1

Chili Pie

Serve with a green salad.

Crust:

500	**mL**	**cooked white rice**	**2**	**cups**
250	**mL**	**grated low-fat Cheddar cheese**	**1**	**cup**
1		**egg, beaten**	**1**	

Filling:

250	**mL**	**chopped onion**	**1**	**cup**
1		**garlic clove, minced**	**1**	
25	**mL**	**canola oil**	**2**	**tbsp.**
250	**mL**	**Laird Lentils**	**1**	**cup**
540	**mL**	**can tomatoes, chopped**	**19**	**oz.**
540	**mL**	**can Kidney Beans**	**19**	**oz.**
7	**mL**	**chili powder**	**1½**	**tsp.**
5	**mL**	**seasoning salt**	**1**	**tsp.**
250	**mL**	**grated low-fat Cheddar cheese**	**1**	**cup**

- Preheat oven to 200°C (400°F).
- Grease a 22 cm (9") pie plate or spray with a nonstick spray.
- To prepare crust, combine rice, cheese and egg. Mix well and press over bottom and sides of pie plate. Bake 20-25 minutes, until firm. Remove from oven.
- Reduce oven temperature to 180°C (350°F).
- In a skillet, sauté onion and garlic in oil until onion is translucent. Add lentils, tomatoes with their juice, beans, chili powder and seasoning salt. Simmer, uncovered, over medium-low heat until liquid is reduced by half, about 40 minutes.
- Spoon filling into pie crust.
- Bake 20-25 minutes, until firm. Sprinkle with cheese and bake 5 minutes or until cheese is melted. Remove from oven, allow to stand 5 minutes, then cut into 6 slices.

6 servings

Questionable Quiche

Beans are user-friendly — pink beans provide the base for "Questionable Quiche."

250	mL	chopped cooked Pink Beans	1	cup
250	mL	chopped zucchini	1	cup
125	mL	chopped onion	½	cup
250	mL	chopped tomato	1	cup
50	mL	grated Parmesan cheese	¼	cup
375	mL	1% milk	1½	cups
175	mL	biscuit mix	¾	cup
3		eggs	3	
2	mL	salt	½	tsp.
1	mL	ground black pepper	¼	tsp.
1		garlic clove, minced	1	
2	mL	dry crumbled basil	½	tsp.
2	mL	dry crumbled parsley	½	tsp.

- Preheat oven to 200°C (400°F).
- Grease a 25 cm (10") quiche pan or pie plate.
- In a bowl, combine beans, zucchini, onion, tomato and cheese.
- In another bowl, combine milk, biscuit mix, eggs, salt, pepper, garlic, basil and parsley. Beat until smooth. Add bean mixture.
- Pour into pan. Bake 35 minutes, or until a knife inserted in centre comes out clean.
- Cool 5 minutes, cut into 8 wedges and serve.

8 servings

Filling Yield:	8 wedges
Serving Size:	1 wedge
Preparation Time:	15 minutes
Pulse Product:	Pink Beans

Nutritional Analysis
(per serving)

Calories:	146	
Total Fat:	5	g
Saturated Fat:	2	g
Protein:	8	g
Carbohydrates:	18	g
Cholesterol:	106	mg
Sodium:	366.5	mg
Potassium:	308	mg
Folic Acid:	19.5	mcg
Total Fiber:	2.5	g
Soluble:	1	g
Insoluble:	1.5	g

Diabetic Food Choices

Protein:	1
Starch:	1
Fats & Oils:	½

Vermicelli Pea Pie

Pulses absorb the flavors of other food, so they can be used in many different ways.

Yield:	2.5 L (10 cups)
Serving Size:	250 mL (1 cup)
Preparation Time:	30 minutes
Pulse Product:	Yellow Split Peas

Nutritional Analysis (per serving)

Calories:	265	
Total Fat:	13	g
Saturated Fat:	3.5	g
Protein:	12	g
Carbohydrates:	25.5	g
Cholesterol:	92.5	mg
Sodium:	234	mg
Potassium:	419	mg
Folic Acid:	17	mcg
Total Fiber:	2	g
Soluble:	1	g
Insoluble:	1	g

Diabetic Food Choices

Protein:	1
Starch:	1½
Fats & Oils:	2

625	mL	cooked vermicelli pasta	2½	cups
25	mL	margarine	2	tbsp.
25	mL	canola oil	2	tbsp.
250	mL	chopped onion	1	cup
250	mL	sliced fresh mushrooms	1	cup
500	mL	cooked Yellow Split Peas	2	cups
25	mL	canola oil	2	tbsp.
375	mL	thinly sliced zucchini	1½	cups
2	mL	dry crumbled basil	½	tsp.
2	mL	ground oregano	½	tsp.
425	mL	low-fat yogurt	1¾	cups
175	mL	grated Edam cheese	¾	cup
3		eggs	3	
2	mL	salt	½	tsp.
2	mL	ground black pepper	½	tsp.
1		large tomato, thinly sliced	1	

- Preheat oven to 180°C (350°F).
- Toss pasta with margarine until coated. Press into deep 23 cm (9") pie plate.
- In a saucepan, heat 25 mL (1 tbsp.) oil over medium heat. Add onion and mushrooms. Sauté until onion is translucent.
- Cover pasta with onion and mushrooms. Top with peas.
- In a saucepan, heat 25 mL (1 tbsp.) oil over medium heat. Add zucchini; stir-fry until softened, about 4 minutes. Add basil and oregano and arrange zucchini over peas.
- Combine yogurt, cheese, eggs, salt and pepper. Mix well. Pour over zucchini.
- Top with tomato slices and bake 45 minutes. Remove from oven. Serve immediately.

10 servings

Manicotti

For a change, try manicotti filled with a Yellow Split Pea mixture.

750	mL	shredded fresh spinach	3	cups
50	mL	margarine	¼	cup
250	mL	chopped onion	1	cup
250	mL	sliced fresh mushrooms	1	cup
500	mL	cooked Yellow Split Peas	2	cups
375	mL	grated low-fat mozzarella cheese	1½	cups
250	mL	low-fat cottage cheese	1	cup
2		eggs, beaten	2	
2	mL	salt	½	tsp.
2	mL	ground black pepper	½	tsp.
12		large manicotti pasta, cooked	12	
2x213	mL	cans mild pizza sauce	2x7½	oz.
50	mL	grated Parmesan cheese	¼	cup

- Preheat oven to 180°C (350°F).
- In a saucepan, cook spinach in boiling water 5 minutes. Remove from heat and drain. Squeeze out excess moisture.
- In a skillet, melt margarine. Add onion and mushrooms. Sauté until onion is translucent.
- Combine spinach, onion, mushrooms, peas, mozzarella cheese, cottage cheese, eggs, salt and pepper. Mix thoroughly.
- Stuff spinach mixture into manicotti noodles. Place pizza sauce in shallow 2 L (2-quart) baking dish. Place filled manicotti in sauce. Sprinkle with Parmesan cheese.
- Cover and bake 45 minutes. Remove from oven and serve.

6 servings

Yield:	12 manicotti
Serving Size:	2 manicotti
Preparation Time:	30 minutes
Pulse Product:	Yellow Split Peas

Nutritional Analysis (per serving)

Calories:	512	
Total Fat:	26	g
Saturated Fat:	8.5	g
Protein:	28	g
Carbohydrates:	42	g
Cholesterol:	117.5	mg
Sodium:	859	mg
Potassium:	683	mg
Folic Acid:	47	mcg
Total Fiber:	2	g
Soluble:	1	g
Insoluble:	1	g

Diabetic Food Choices

Protein:	2½
Starch:	2
Fruit & Vegetables:	1
Fats & Oils:	3½

Yield:	12 pieces
Serving Size:	1 pieces
Preparation Time:	25 minutes
Pulse Product:	Pinto Beans

Nutritional Analysis
(per serving)

Calories:	184	
Total Fat:	6	g
Saturated Fat:	3	g
Protein:	12.5	g
Carbohydrates:	22	g
Cholesterol:	36	mg
Sodium:	440	mg
Potassium:	519	mg
Folic Acid:	34.5	mcg
Total Fiber:	3	g
Soluble:	1.5	g
Insoluble:	1.5	g

Diabetic Food Choices

Protein:	1½
Starch:	1
Fruit & Vegetables:	½

Beany Lasagne

Meatless lasagne.

175	mL	chopped onion	¾	cup
125	mL	diced celery	½	cup
125	mL	diced green pepper	½	cup
2		garlic cloves, minced	2	
15	mL	canola oil	1	tbsp.
796	mL	can tomatoes	28	oz.
156	mL	can tomato paste	5½	oz.
500	mL	cooked Pinto Beans	2	cups
125	mL	sliced fresh mushrooms	½	cup
15	mL	dry crumbled parsley	1	tbsp.
2	mL	dry crumbled oregano	½	tsp.
2	mL	dry crumbled basil	½	tsp.
2	mL	granulated sugar	½	tsp.
5	mL	salt	1	tsp.
1	mL	ground black pepper	¼	tsp.
250	mL	low-fat cottage cheese	1	cup
1		egg, beaten	1	
8		cooked lasagne noodles	8	
500	mL	grated low-fat mozzarella cheese	2	cups

- In a skillet, sauté onion, celery, pepper and garlic in oil until onion is translucent.
- Add tomatoes, tomato paste, beans, mushrooms, herbs and spices.
- Cover and bring to a boil. Reduce heat and simmer 1 hour, stirring occasionally.
- Preheat oven to 180°C (350°F).
- In a bowl, combine cottage cheese and egg.
- Spread a layer of tomato sauce in a 22 x 34 cm (9 x 13") baking pan. Cover with half of the noodles, then a layer of cottage cheese mixture. Repeat each layer, ending with sauce. Sprinkle grated cheese on top.
- Bake 45-55 minutes, or until heated. Let stand 15 minutes before serving. Cut into 12 pieces.

12 servings

Hawaiian Split Peas and Tuna

This tastes great served with Rose Lentils and Rice on page 95.

500 mL	cooked Yellow Split Peas	2	cups
120 g	can water-packed tuna, drained	4.23	oz.
284 mL	can cream of chicken soup	10	oz.
125 mL	coconut milk	½	cup
5 mL	curry powder	1	tsp.
540 mL	can crushed pineapple, drained	19	oz.
75 mL	salted cashews	⅓	cup

- Preheat oven to 180°C (350°F).
- In a bowl, combine peas, tuna, soup, coconut milk, curry powder and pineapple.
- Spray a 1.5 L (1½-quart) casserole with non-stick vegetable spray. Pour tuna mixture into the casserole; cover and bake 30 minutes.
- Remove cover; sprinkle cashews on top and bake another 10 minutes, uncovered.

8 servings

Yield:	1 L (4 cups)
Serving Size:	125 mL (½ cup)
Preparation Time:	10 minutes
Pulse Product:	Yellow Split Peas

Nutritional Analysis (per serving)

Calories:	342	
Total Fat:	11	g
Saturated Fat:	4	g
Protein:	18.5	g
Carbohydrates:	45.5	g
Cholesterol:	15	mg
Sodium:	886	mg
Potassium:	607	mg
Folic Acid:	13	mcg
Total Fiber:	4	g
Soluble:	1	g
Insoluble:	3	g

Diabetic Food Choices

Protein:	2
Starch:	1½
Sugar:	1½
Fats & Oils:	1

Baked Stuffed Sole

To butterfly a fillet, slit the fillet, lengthwise, down the side, almost through so that there is a pocket in the fillet for the stuffing.

454	**g**	**sole fillets (2 large)**	**1 lb.**
50	**mL**	**margarine**	**¼ cup**
125	**mL**	**diced carrot**	**½ cup**
125	**mL**	**diced onion**	**½ cup**
250	**mL**	**cooked Yellow Split Peas**	**1 cup**
2	**mL**	**dry crumbled marjoram**	**½ tsp.**
2	**mL**	**dry crumbled basil**	**½ tsp.**
2	**mL**	**salt**	**½ tsp.**
1	**mL**	**ground black pepper**	**¼ tsp.**
50	**mL**	**dried bread crumbs**	**¼ cup**
125	**mL**	**grated low-fat mozzarella cheese paprika**	**½ cup**

- Preheat oven to 200°C (400°F).
- Wash fillets and pat dry. Cut each large fillet almost in half horizontally, butterfly-style.
- In a saucepan, melt margarine. Pour off half and reserve.
- To the remaining melted margarine, add carrot and onion. Sauté 5 minutes, or until tender. Add peas, marjoram, basil, salt and pepper. Stir and sauté 2 minutes over medium heat.
- Remove from heat, stir in bread crumbs and cheese.
- Divide filling in half and spoon into fillets. Close and secure each fillet with a toothpick.
- Place in shallow nonstick baking dish. Drizzle with reserved margarine and sprinkle with paprika.
- Bake 20 minutes. Remove from oven, halve each fillet vertically and serve immediately.

4 servings

Yield: 500 mL (2 cups)

Serving Size: ½ fillet stuffed with 125 mL (½ cup) filling

Preparation Time: 25 minutes

Pulse Product: Yellow Split Peas

Nutritional Analysis
(per serving)

Calories:	519	
Total Fat:	30.5	g
Saturated Fat:	7	g
Protein:	38	g
Carbohydrates:	22.5	g
Cholesterol:	72	mg
Sodium:	732	mg
Potassium:	629	mg
Folic Acid:	17.5	mcg
Total Fiber:	2	g
Soluble:	1	g
Insoluble:	1	g

Diabetic Food Choices

Protein:	4
Starch:	½
Skim Milk:	2

Pictured on page 53.

Chicken Stir-Fry

A quick stir-fry for busy nights.

Orange Soy Sauce:

125	mL	light chicken broth*	½	cup
25	mL	orange juice	2	tbsp.
15	mL	white vinegar	1	tbsp.
5	mL	ground ginger	1	tsp.
25	mL	sodium-reduced soy sauce*	2	tbsp.
25	mL	cornstarch	2	tbsp.
15	mL	granulated sugar	1	tbsp.
1		garlic clove, minced	1	
454	g	skinless, boneless chicken breasts	1	lb.
25	mL	canola oil	2	tbsp.
125	mL	diced carrot	½	cup
125	mL	diced celery	½	cup
125	mL	bamboo shoots	½	cup
125	mL	snow peas	½	cup
125	mL	water chestnuts	½	cup
125	mL	mini corn cobs	½	cup
500	mL	cooked Yellow Split Peas (just until tender)	2	cups
500	mL	fresh bean sprouts	2	cups

- In a bowl, combine chicken broth, orange juice, vinegar, ginger, soy sauce, cornstarch, sugar and garlic. Mix well and set aside.
- Cut chicken breasts into small pieces.
- In a large nonstick skillet or wok, heat oil over high heat. Add chicken and stir-fry 5 minutes, or until cooked.
- Add carrot, celery and bamboo shoots, stir-fry 2-3 minutes. Add snow peas, water chestnuts and corn cobs, stir-fry 2 minutes.
- Add peas and bean sprouts, stir-fry 1 minute, or until vegetables are tender-crisp.
- Add sauce and heat until it begins to thicken.
- Remove from heat and serve immediately.

6 servings

*Gluten-free brand required

Gluten-Free

Yield:	1.5 L (6 cups)
Serving Size:	250 mL (1 cup)
Preparation Time:	25 minutes
Pulse Product:	Yellow Split Peas

Nutritional Analysis
(per serving)

Calories:	290	
Total Fat:	7	g
Saturated Fat:	1	g
Protein:	29	g
Carbohydrates:	28.5	g
Cholesterol:	48	mg
Sodium:	184	mg
Potassium:	731.5	mg
Folic Acid:	23.5	mcg
Total Fiber:	3	g
Soluble:	1	g
Insoluble:	2	g

Diabetic Food Choices

Protein:	3½
Starch:	1
Fruit & Vegetables:	½

Filling Yield:	8 wedges
Serving Size:	1 wedge
Preparation Time:	30 minutes
Pulse Product:	Yellow Split Peas

Nutritional Analysis
(per serving)

Calories:	299	
Total Fat:	13	g
Saturated Fat:	5.5	g
Protein:	17	g
Carbohydrates:	28.5	g
Cholesterol:	70	mg
Sodium:	823.5	mg
Potassium:	409	mg
Folic Acid:	11.5	mcg
Total Fiber:	2	g
Soluble:	1	g
Insoluble:	1	g

Diabetic Food Choices

Protein:	1
Starch:	1
Skim Milk:	1
Fruit & Vegetables:	½
Fats & Oils:	2

Pea-zza

Pizza with a difference — a split pea difference!

625	mL	cooked long-grain rice	2½	cups
125	mL	grated low-fat Cheddar cheese	½	cup
1		egg, beaten	1	
500	mL	cooked Yellow Split Peas	2	cups
175	mL	diced tomato	¾	cup
213	mL	can tomato sauce*	7½	oz.
2	mL	dry crumbled oregano	½	tsp.
2	mL	dry crumbled basil	½	tsp.
2	mL	ground black pepper	½	tsp.
1		garlic clove, minced	1	
175	mL	diced pepperoni*	¾	cup
50	mL	diced onion	¼	cup
50	mL	diced sweet red pepper	¼	cup
250	mL	grated low-fat mozzarella cheese	1	cup

- Preheat oven to 200°C (400°F).
- In a bowl, combine rice, Cheddar cheese and egg. Mix and press into a 30 cm (12") pizza pan. Bake 5 minutes.
- In a bowl, combine peas, tomato, tomato sauce, oregano, basil, ground pepper and garlic. Mix well. Spread on crust.
- Top with pepperoni, onion and pepper.
- Top with mozzarella cheese.
- Bake 30 minutes.
- Remove from oven and let stand 5 minutes. Slice into 8 wedges and serve.

8 servings

*Gluten-free brand required

Lentil Pizza Squares

Teenagers love this!

50	mL	canola oil	¼	cup
175	mL	chopped onion	¾	cup
250	mL	sliced fresh mushrooms	1	cup
1		garlic clove, minced	1	
4		eggs	4	
375	mL	Rose Lentil purée	1½	cups
375	mL	low-fat sour cream*	1½	cups
213	mL	can tomato sauce*	7½	oz.
175	mL	cornmeal	¾	cup
5	mL	dry crumbled basil	1	tsp.
5	mL	dry crumbled oregano	1	tsp.
2	mL	salt	½	tsp.
375	mL	grated low-fat Cheddar cheese	1½	cups
375	mL	grated low-fat mozzarella cheese	1½	cups
125	mL	sliced pepperoni*	½	cup
125	mL	sliced ripe olives	½	cup
125	mL	diced sweet green pepper	½	cup

- Preheat oven to 180°C (350°F).
- In a skillet, heat oil and add onion, mushrooms and garlic. Sauté until onion is translucent. Remove from heat and let cool.
- In a large mixing bowl, beat eggs. Blend in lentil purée, sour cream, tomato sauce, cornmeal, basil, oregano, salt and mushroom mixture. Stir in cheeses.
- Turn into a 22 x 34 cm (9 x 13") baking dish sprayed with nonstick vegetable spray.
- Garnish with pepperoni, olives and pepper.
- Bake 40-45 minutes, or until firm to touch. Let stand 10 minutes before cutting. Cut into 12 squares.
- **12 servings.**

*Gluten-free brand required

Gluten-Free

Yield:	12 squares
Serving Size:	1 square
Preparation Time:	40 minutes
Pulse Product:	Rose Lentils

Nutritional Analysis
(per serving)

Calories:	293	
Total Fat:	18.5	g
Saturated Fat:	7	g
Protein:	15	g
Carbohydrates:	18	g
Cholesterol:	141	mg
Sodium:	784.5	mg
Potassium:	313	mg
Folic Acid:	19.5	mcg
Total Fiber:	1.5	g
Soluble:	0.5	g
Insoluble:	1	g

Diabetic Food Choices

Protein:	2
Starch:	1
Fats & Oils:	2½

122

Mexican Salad Bowl, page 85
Spicy Pea and Pork Tamale Pie, page 128

Yield:	175 L (7 cups)
Serving Size:	250 mL (1 cup)
Preparation Time:	30 minutes
Pulse Product:	Great Northern Beans

Nutritional Analysis
(per serving)

Calories:	377	
Total Fat:	10.5	g
Saturated Fat:	2.5	g
Protein:	14	g
Carbohydrates:	57	g
Cholesterol:	62.5	mg
Sodium:	371	mg
Potassium:	650	mg
Folic Acid:	23.5	mcg
Total Fiber:	6	g
Soluble:	3	g
Insoluble:	3	g

Diabetic Food Choices

Protein:	1
Starch:	2½
Fruit & Vegetables:	1½
Fats & Oils:	1½

Italian Super Supper

Double this recipe to feed a hungry crowd.

500	mL	pasta (penne OR rotini)	2	cups
1	kg	smoked garlic sausage	2.2	lbs.
1		large onion, chopped	1	
2		garlic cloves, minced	2	
500	mL	sliced fresh mushrooms	2	cups
25	mL	canola oil	2	tbsp.
796	mL	can Italian seasoned tomatoes	28	oz.
500	mL	cooked Great Northern Beans	2	cups
2	mL	dry crumbled chili peppers	½	tsp.
2	mL	dry crumbled oregano	½	tsp.
2	mL	dry crumbled basil	½	tsp.

- Cook pasta according to package directions. Drain and set aside.
- Steam sausage then brown in skillet. Remove sausage and drain off fat. Cut sausage into 1 cm (½") thick pieces.
- In a large saucepan, sauté onion, garlic and mushrooms in oil for 5 minutes. Add tomatoes, beans, chilies, oregano and basil. Add pasta and sausage. Stir thoroughly until heated through.

7 servings

Lentil Italiano

Easy to prepare and the whole family will enjoy it.

454 g	**mild Italian sausage, steamed**	**1**	**lb.**
125 mL	**chopped onion**	**½**	**cup**
500 mL	**cooked Laird Lentils**	**2**	**cups**
75 mL	**all-purpose flour**	**⅓**	**cup**
	pinch of garlic powder		
540 mL	**can tomatoes**	**19**	**oz.**
250 mL	**grated low-fat mozzarella cheese**	**1**	**cup**

- Preheat oven to 180°C (350°F).
- In a skillet, brown sausage on both sides, 10-15 minutes.
- Slice sausage into rounds. Place into a 2 L (2-quart) casserole.
- In a skillet, sauté onion until soft.
- Add lentils, flour, garlic powder, tomatoes and onion to the casserole.
- Top with mozzarella cheese.
- Bake 30-40 minutes.

6 servings

Yield:	1.5 L (6 cups)
Serving Size:	250 mL (1 cup)
Preparation Time:	30 minutes
Pulse Product:	Laird Lentils

Nutritional Analysis
(per serving)

Calories:	509	
Total Fat:	37.5	g
Saturated Fat:	17	g
Protein:	22	g
Carbohydrates:	24.5	g
Cholesterol:	68	mg
Sodium:	775.5	mg
Potassium:	564	mg
Folic Acid:	29	mcg
Total Fiber:	7	g
Soluble:	2	g
Insoluble:	0.5	g

Diabetic Food Choices

Protein:	2½
Starch:	1
Fruit & Vegetables:	½
Fats & Oils:	6

Yield:	1 L (4 cups)
Serving Size:	125 mL (½ cup)
Preparation Time:	25 minutes
Pulse Product:	Eston Lentils

Nutritional Analysis
(per serving)

Calories:	452	
Total Fat:	33	g
Saturated Fat:	14	g
Protein:	11.5	g
Carbohydrates:	31	g
Cholesterol:	38	mg
Sodium:	504	mg
Potassium:	481.5	mg
Folic Acid:	27.5	mcg
Total Fiber:	7	g
Soluble:	1.5	g
Insoluble:	5.5	g

Diabetic Food Choices

Protein:	1½
Starch:	1
Sugar:	2
Fats & Oils:	5

Pork and Lentils

Pork and beans redone with lentils.

454	g	lean side bacon, chopped*	1	lb.
750	mL	cooked Eston Lentils	3	cups
250	mL	diced onion	1	cup
50	mL	molasses	¼	cup
50	mL	brown sugar	¼	cup
50	mL	ketchup*	¼	cup
50	mL	water	¼	cup
15	mL	Worcestershire sauce*	1	tbsp.
25	mL	white vinegar	2	tbsp.

- In a skillet, fry bacon until crisp. Remove bacon, place on paper toweling and pat until excess fat has been removed.
- In a large saucepan or Dutch oven, combine bacon, lentils, onion, molasses, brown sugar, ketchup, water and Worcestershire sauce. Bring to a boil. Reduce heat, cover and simmer 15 minutes, or until onions are done.
- Stir in vinegar. Serve.

8 servings

*Gluten-free brand required

Spicy Pea and Pork Tamale Pie

Peas and pork, a great combination.

250	mL	cornmeal	1	cup
5	mL	salt	1	tsp.
250	mL	cold water	1	cup
500	mL	boiling water	2	cups
227	g	lean ground pork	½	lb.
125	mL	chopped onion	½	cup
2		garlic cloves, minced	2	
375	mL	cooked Yellow Split Peas	1½	cups
25	mL	all purpose flour	2	tbsp.
398	mL	can Mexican stewed tomatoes, chopped	14	oz.
10	mL	chili powder	2	tsp.
2	mL	dry crumbled oregano	½	tsp.
1		sweet red pepper, cut in rings	1	
125	mL	diced low-fat Cheddar cheese	½	cup

- Preheat oven to 180°C (350°F).
- In a saucepan, combine cornmeal, salt and cold water. Slowly add boiling water, stirring constantly. Cook until thickened, stirring frequently. Cover and continue cooking over low heat 5 minutes.
- Spread cornmeal mixture in a greased 22 x 34 cm (9 x 13") pan.
- In a skillet, brown pork, onion and garlic. Drain off excess fat. Stir in peas and flour.
- Add tomatoes and their juice, chili powder and oregano. Mix well. Pour over cornmeal.
- Garnish with pepper rings and cheese.
- Bake 20 minutes. Cut into 12 pieces.

12 servings

Yield:	12 pieces
Serving Size:	1 piece
Preparation Time:	45 minutes
Pulse Product:	Yellow Split Peas

Nutritional Analysis
(per serving)

Calories:	128	
Total Fat:	2	g
Saturated Fat:	1	g
Protein:	8	g
Carbohydrates:	19	g
Cholesterol:	18	mg
Sodium:	273.5	mg
Potassium:	239.5	mg
Folic Acid:	5.5	mcg
Total Fiber:	1.5	g
Soluble:	0.5	g
Insoluble:	1	g

Diabetic Food Choices

| Protein: | 1 |
| Starch: | 1 |

Pictured on page 123.

<table>
<tr><td>Yield:</td><td>6 wedges</td></tr>
<tr><td>Serving Size:</td><td>1 wedge</td></tr>
<tr><td>Preparation Time:</td><td>30 minutes</td></tr>
<tr><td>Pulse Product:</td><td>Pink Beans</td></tr>
</table>

Nutritional Analysis
(per serving)

Calories:	455	
Total Fat:	22	g
Saturated Fat:	7	g
Protein:	29.5	g
Carbohydrates:	36	g
Cholesterol:	164	mg
Sodium:	2059.5	mg
Potassium:	781	mg
Folic Acid:	28	mcg
Total Fiber:	8	g
Soluble:	2	g
Insoluble:	6	g

Diabetic Food Choices

Protein:	4
Starch:	2
Fats & Oils:	2

Upside Down Tamale Pie

To make as hot as you want; add more chili.

454	g	lean ground beef	1	lb.
75	mL	chopped onion	⅓	cup
2		garlic cloves, minced	2	
25	mL	all-purpose flour	2	tbsp.
125	mL	sliced, pitted ripe olives	½	cup
540	mL	can tomatoes, chopped	19	oz.
10	mL	chili powder	2	tsp.
250	mL	cooked Pink Beans	1	cup
0.5	mL	dry crumbled chili pepper	⅛	tsp.
		salt and ground black pepper to taste		
125	mL	cubed low-fat Cheddar cheese	½	cup

Cornmeal Crust:

250	mL	cornmeal	1	cup
500	mL	1% milk	2	cups
15	mL	canola oil	1	tbsp.
5	mL	salt	1	tsp.
2		eggs	2	

- In a skillet, brown ground beef. Drain off excess fat. Add onion and garlic; cook until soft.
- Add flour, olives, tomatoes and juice, chili powder, beans, chili pepper, salt and pepper. Simmer 15 minutes.
- Pour into a 2 L (2-quart) casserole. Top with cheese.
- Preheat oven to 180°C (350°F).
- In a saucepan, combine cornmeal, milk, oil, salt and eggs. Heat over medium heat until thickened, stirring frequently.
- Cover meat with cornmeal. Bake 20 minutes, until bubbly. Cut into 6 wedges.

6 servings

Spicy Lentil Meat Loaf

An old favorite with added fiber.

454	g	lean ground beef	1	lb.
1	L	cooked Eston Lentils	4	cups
175	mL	chopped sweet red pepper	¾	cup
250	mL	water	1	cup
125	mL	ketchup*	½	cup
45	g	pkg. French onion soup mix*	1½	oz.
5	mL	prepared mustard*	1	tsp.
5	mL	white vinegar	1	tsp.
		sprigs of fresh parsley		

- Preheat oven to 180°C (350°F).
- In a skillet, brown ground beef. Drain off excess fat.
- In a 3 L (3-quart) casserole, combine beef, lentils, sweet pepper, water, ketchup, soup mix, mustard and vinegar.
- Bake 30 minutes. Garnish with parsley.

8 servings

*Gluten-free brand required

Gluten-Free

Yield:	2 L (8 cups)
Serving Size:	250 mL (1 cup)
Preparation Time:	15 minutes
Pulse Product:	Eston Lentils

Nutritional Analysis (per serving)

Calories:	236	
Total Fat:	7	g
Saturated Fat:	3	g
Protein:	22	g
Carbohydrates:	27	g
Cholesterol:	42	mg
Sodium:	451	mg
Potassium:	571.5	mg
Folic Acid:	37	mcg
Total Fiber:	9	g
Soluble:	2	g
Insoluble:	7	g

Diabetic Food Choices

Protein:	2½
Starch:	1
Fruit & Vegetables:	½

Yield:	1.25 L
	(5 cups)
Serving Size:	250 mL
	(1 cup)
Preparation Time:	15 minutes
Pulse Product:	Laird Lentils

Nutritional Analysis
(per serving)

Calories:	257	
Total Fat:	11	g
Saturated Fat:	5	g
Protein:	26	g
Carbohydrates:	17	g
Cholesterol:	67	mg
Sodium:	420	mg
Potassium:	755	mg
Folic Acid:	24	mcg
Total Fiber:	5	g
Soluble:	1	g
Insoluble:	4	g

Diabetic Food Choices

Protein:	3½
Starch:	1

Lentil Chili Con Carne

Lentils help to stretch the meat as well as adding fiber in this recipe.

454	g	lean ground beef	1	lb.
1		medium onion, chopped	1	
1		garlic clove, minced	1	
540	mL	can tomato sauce	19	oz.
250	mL	cooked Laird Lentils	1	cup
284	mL	can whole mushrooms, drained	10	oz.
125	mL	water	½	cup
15	mL	chili powder	1	tbsp.
2	mL	ground black pepper	½	tsp.
15	mL	white vinegar	1	tbsp.

- In a heavy skillet, brown beef with onion and garlic. Drain off excess fat.
- Add tomato sauce, lentils, mushrooms, water, chili powder and pepper. Bring to a boil, reduce heat and simmer, covered, 1 hour.
- Add vinegar and simmer 15 minutes.
  5 servings

Mexican Split Pea Hash

A nutritious supper in 20 minutes.

15	mL	canola oil	1 tbsp.
125	mL	finely diced onion	½ cup
2		garlic cloves, minced	2
75	mL	raisins	⅓ cup
75	mL	apple juice	⅓ cup
25	mL	red wine vinegar	2 tbsp.
5	mL	chili powder	1 tsp.
2	mL	cinnamon	½ tsp.
1	mL	cumin	¼ tsp.
1	mL	ground cloves	¼ tsp.
250	mL	cooked Yellow Split Peas, just until tender	1 cup
250	mL	finely diced roast beef	1 cup
125	mL	chili sauce	½ cup
2	mL	salt	½ tsp.
2	mL	ground black pepper	½ tsp.
75	mL	slivered almonds	⅓ cup
2		hard-cooked eggs, peeled and chopped	2

- In a skillet, heat oil and sauté onion and garlic 3 minutes.
- Add raisins, apple juice, vinegar, chili powder, cinnamon, cumin and cloves. Cook mixture until syrupy.
- Add peas, beef, chili sauce, salt and pepper. Cook over low heat until heated through.
- Remove from heat. Stir in almonds and eggs.
- Serve on top of cooked orzo pasta or rice.

6 servings

Yield:	750 mL (3 cups)
Serving Size:	125 mL (½ cup)
Preparation Time:	20 minutes
Pulse Product:	Yellow Split Peas

Nutritional Analysis (per serving)

Calories:	266	
Total Fat:	12.5	g
Saturated Fat:	3	g
Protein:	15	g
Carbohydrates:	25	g
Cholesterol:	124.5	g
Sodium:	221	mg
Potassium:	546	mg
Folic Acid:	12.5	mcg
Total Fiber:	2	g
Soluble:	1	g
Insoluble:	1	g

Diabetic Food Choices

Protein:	2
Starch:	1½
Fats & Oils:	1

Yield:	2.25 L (9 cups)
Serving Size:	250 mL (1 cup)
Preparation Time:	30 minutes
Pulse Product:	Laird Lentils

Nutritional Analysis
(per serving)

Calories:	225	
Total Fat:	7	g
Saturated Fat:	3	g
Protein:	16	g
Carbohydrates:	27	g
Cholesterol:	37	mg
Sodium:	572	mg
Potassium:	775	mg
Folic Acid:	37.5	mcg
Total Fiber:	6	g
Soluble:	2.5	g
Insoluble:	3.5	g

Diabetic Food Choices

Protein:	2
Fruit & Vegetables:	2

Saskamongo

For people on the go!

454	g	lean ground beef	1	lb.
540	mL	can tomatoes	19	oz.
500	mL	water	2	cups
284	mL	can tomato soup*	10	oz.
250	mL	cooked Laird Lentils	1	cup
250	mL	frozen peas	1	cup
4		carrots, diced	4	
4		parsnips, diced	4	
4		celery stalks, diced	4	
0.5		sweet green pepper, diced	½	
2		garlic cloves, minced	2	
1		bay leaf	1	
2	mL	salt	½	tsp.
2	mL	dry crumbled basil	½	tsp.
1	mL	ground black pepper	¼	tsp.

- Preheat oven to 180°C (350°F).
- In a skillet, brown ground beef, drain off excess fat.
- In a 3 L (3-quart) casserole, combine beef, tomatoes, water, tomato soup, lentils, peas, carrots, parsnips, celery, sweet pepper, garlic, bay leaf, salt, basil and black pepper. Bake 1 hour.

9 servings

*Gluten-free brand required

LOAVES, BUNS & MUFFINS

Best Ever Pecan Bread

Pecans add extra crunch to this quick bread.

75 mL	shortening	⅓	cup
375 mL	granulated sugar	1½	cups
2	eggs	2	
250 mL	Yellow Split Pea purée	1	cup
75 mL	water	⅓	cup
375 mL	all-purpose flour	1½	cups
5 mL	baking soda	1	tsp.
2 mL	salt	½	tsp.
1 mL	baking powder	¼	tsp.
5 mL	cinnamon	1	tsp.
2 mL	nutmeg	½	tsp.
250 mL	chopped pecans	1	cup

- Preheat oven to 180°C (350°F).
- In a bowl, cream shortening and sugar. Add eggs, 1 at a time, beating well. Stir in purée and water.
- In a separate bowl, mix together flour, baking soda, salt, baking powder, cinnamon and nutmeg.
- Add dry ingredients to wet ingredients. Mix thoroughly. Add pecans.
- Pour into a greased and floured 13 x 23 cm (5 x 9") loaf pan. Bake 60-70 minutes.
- Turn out on a rack and cool. Cut into 15 slices.
- **15 servings**

Yield:	15 slices
Serving Size:	1 slice
Preparation Time:	20 minutes
Pulse Product:	Yellow Split Peas

Nutritional Analysis
(per serving)

Calories:	256	
Total Fat:	10	g
Saturated Fat:	1.5	g
Protein:	4	g
Carbohydrates:	39.5	g
Cholesterol:	36.5	mg
Sodium:	175	mg
Potassium:	102	mg
Folic Acid:	8	mcg
Total Fiber:	1.5	g
Soluble:	0.5	g
Insoluble:	1	g

Diabetic Food Choices

Starch:	2
Sugar:	1
Fats & Oils:	2

Yield:	36 buns
Serving Size:	1 bun
Preparation Time:	45 minutes
Pulse Product:	Pink Beans

Nutritional Analysis
(per serving)

Calories:	141	
Total Fat:	2	g
Saturated Fat:	trace	
Protein:	3.5	g
Carbohydrates:	27	g
Cholesterol:	1.5	mg
Sodium:	44	mg
Potassium:	121	mg
Folic Acid:	16.5	mcg
Total Fiber:	1	g
Soluble:	0.5	g
Insoluble:	0.5	g

Diabetic Food Choices

Starch:	1½
Skim Milk:	½
Fats & Oils:	½

Sweet Bean Buns

Enhanced hot cross buns.

500	mL	scalded milk, cooled to lukewarm	2	cups
50	mL	granulated sugar	¼	cup
25	mL	dry yeast (14 g)	2	tbsp.
500	mL	Pink Bean purée	2	cups
2	mL	salt	½	tsp.
50	mL	canola oil	¼	cup
250	mL	raisins	1	cup
150	mL	fruit peel (optional)	⅔	cup
10	mL	cinnamon	2	tsp.
1.25-1.5	L	all-purpose flour	5-6	cups
		vanilla icing		

- In a large bowl, combine milk, sugar and yeast; let rise 5 minutes.
- In a bowl, mix bean purée, salt, oil, raisins, fruit peel and cinnamon; add to yeast mixture. Stir in up to 1.5 L (6 cups) flour to form a soft dough. (Add enough flour so the dough handles easily.)
- Turn the dough onto a floured surface and knead until smooth and elastic. Place dough in a greased bowl; lightly oil top of dough. Cover and let rise in a warm place until dough is double in size, approximately 1 hour.
- Punch down; cover. Let dough rise again until almost double in size. Punch down.
- Preheat oven to 180°C (350°F).
- Divide dough into egg-sized buns. Place on a greased cookie sheet. Cover and let rise until double in size, about 45 minutes.
- Bake 25-30 minutes.
- When cool, make an "x" shape on the bun with vanilla icing.

36 servings

Carrot Nut Muffins

If you prefer a loaf, turn batter into 2, 13 x 23 cm (5 x 9") loaf pans and bake 55 minutes.

500	mL	all-purpose flour	2	cups
10	mL	baking soda	2	tsp.
7	mL	baking powder	1½	tsp.
5	mL	salt	1	tsp.
10	mL	cinnamon	2	tsp.
5	mL	ground cloves	1	tsp.
5	mL	ground allspice	1	tsp.
500	mL	granulated sugar	2	cups
250	mL	canola oil	1	cup
4		eggs	4	
500	mL	grated carrot	2	cups
250	mL	Laird Lentil purée	1	cup
250	mL	chopped walnuts	1	cup

- Preheat oven to 180°C (350°F).
- In a large bowl, combine flour, baking soda, baking powder, salt, cinnamon, cloves and allspice.
- In a small bowl, combine sugar, oil and eggs. Add to flour mixture.
- Mix together carrot, lentil purée and walnuts. Add to flour mixture. Mix well.
- Spoon batter into lined or greased medium-sized muffin tins filling ¾ full.
- Bake 30 minutes, or until toothpick inserted in center comes out clean.

36 servings

Yield:	36 muffins or 2 loaves
Serving Size:	1 muffin
Preparation Time:	30 minutes
Pulse Product:	Laird Lentils

Nutritional Analysis (per serving)

Calories:	176	
Total Fat:	9	g
Saturated Fat:	1	g
Protein:	2.5	g
Carbohydrates:	23	g
Cholesterol:	30.5	mg
Sodium:	147.5	mg
Potassium:	79	mg
Folic Acid:	6	mcg
Total Fiber:	1	g
Soluble:	0.5	g
Insoluble:	0.5	g

Diabetic Food Choices

Starch:	½
Sugar:	1½
Fats & Oils:	2

Yield:	12 muffins
Serving Size:	1 muffin
Preparation Time:	25 minutes
Pulse Product:	Pinto Beans

Nutritional Analysis
(per serving)

Calories:	190	
Total Fat:	5.5	g
Saturated Fat:	1	g
Protein:	4	g
Carbohydrates:	32	g
Cholesterol:	23.5	mg
Sodium:	95	mg
Potassium:	189	mg
Folic Acid:	17	mcg
Total Fiber:	2	g
Soluble:	1	g
Insoluble:	1	g

Diabetic Food Choices

Starch:	2
Fats & Oils:	1

Spicy Bean Muffins

Power-packed muffins.

250	mL	cooked Pinto Beans	1	cup
175	mL	juice from 1 orange plus milk to equal	¾	cup
1		egg	1	
50	mL	canola oil	¼	cup
125	mL	brown sugar, packed	½	cup
375	mL	all-purpose flour	1½	cups
10	mL	baking powder	2	tsp.
5	mL	cinnamon	1	tsp.
125	mL	chopped dates	½	cup

- Preheat oven to 200°C (400°F).
- In a blender, purée beans with orange juice and milk until smooth.
- Pour mixture into mixing bowl. Beat in egg, oil and brown sugar.
- In a bowl, combine flour, baking powder, cinnamon and dates.
- Fold into bean mixture, mixing just until dry ingredients are moistened.
- Spoon into greased or paper-lined, medium-sized muffin tins filling ¾ full. Bake 15-18 minutes.

12 servings

Maggie's Muffins

Makes a large batch of wonderful moist muffins.

175	mL	raisins	¾	cup
175	mL	chopped dates	¾	cup
375	mL	water	1½	cups
250	mL	Eston Lentil purée	1	cup
125	mL	margarine	½	cup
175	mL	brown sugar	¾	cup
1		egg	1	
5	mL	vanilla	1	tsp.
375	mL	all-purpose flour	1½	cups
5	mL	baking powder	1	tsp.
5	mL	baking soda	1	tsp.
1	mL	salt	¼	tsp.

- Preheat oven to 180°C (350°F).
- In a heavy saucepan, combine raisins, dates and water. Simmer 20 minutes, stirring occasionally. Cool 10 minutes.
- Add lentil purée to raisin mixture and mix well.
- In a bowl, cream together margarine and sugar. Beat in egg and vanilla. Add raisin-lentil mixture.
- In another bowl, combine flour, baking powder, baking soda and salt.
- Stir into fruit mixture. Mix until just combined.
- Fill lined or greased medium-sized muffin tins ¾ full.
- Bake 20-25 minutes, or until toothpick inserted in center comes out clean.

24 servings

Yield:	24 muffins
Serving Size:	1 muffin
Preparation Time:	25 minutes
Pulse Product:	Eston Lentils

Nutritional Analysis
(per serving)

Calories:	133	
Total Fat:	4.5	g
Saturated Fat:	1	g
Protein:	2	g
Carbohydrates:	22.5	g
Cholesterol:	11.5	mg
Sodium:	144.5	mg
Potassium:	128	mg
Folic Acid:	5	mcg
Total Fiber:	1.5	g
Soluble:	0.5	g
Insoluble:	1	g

Diabetic Food Choices

Starch:	1
Fruit & Vegetables:	½
Fats & Oils:	1

Yield:	24 muffins
Serving Size:	1 muffin
Preparation Time:	25 minutes
Pulse Product:	Laird Lentils

Nutritional Analysis
(per serving)

Calories:	218	
Total Fat:	4	g
Saturated Fat:	trace	
Protein:	4	g
Carbohydrates:	45	g
Cholesterol:	11.5	mg
Sodium:	218	mg
Potassium:	392	mg
Folic Acid:	10	mcg
Total Fiber:	2.5	g
Soluble:	0.5	g
Insoluble:	2	g

Diabetic Food Choices

Starch:	2
Fruit & Vegetables:	½
Sugar:	½
Fats & Oils:	½

Lentil, Bran and Date Muffins

A high-fiber, low-fat muffin.

300	mL	all-purpose flour	1¼	cups
250	mL	whole-wheat flour	1	cup
250	mL	bran	1	cup
15	mL	baking powder	1	tbsp.
7	mL	baking soda	1½	tsp.
2	mL	cinnamon	½	tsp.
2	mL	salt	½	tsp.
1		egg	1	
355	mL	can frozen apple juice concentrate	12½	oz.
125	mL	milk	½	cup
75	mL	canola oil	⅓	cup
50	mL	packed brown sugar	¼	cup
500	mL	rice crisp cereal	2	cups
375	mL	chopped dates	1½	cups
250	mL	Laird Lentil purée	1	cup

- Preheat oven to 190°C (375°F).
- In a large bowl, stir together flours, bran, baking powder, soda, cinnamon and salt.
- In a separate bowl, beat together egg, apple juice concentrate, milk, oil and sugar.
- Stir in cereal, dates and purée. Stir into dry ingredients just until moistened.
- Spoon into large greased or paper-lined medium-sized muffin tins filling ¾ full.
- Bake 20 minutes, or until toothpick inserted in center comes out clean.

24 servings

Lentil Bran Muffins

Breakfast on the run!

250	mL	buttermilk	1	cup
500	mL	bran flakes	2	cups
625	mL	all-purpose flour	2½	cups
15	mL	baking soda	1	tbsp.
2	mL	salt	½	tsp.
125	mL	canola oil	½	cup
250	mL	granulated sugar	1	cup
2		eggs	2	
125	mL	raisins	½	cup
625	mL	Laird Lentil purée	2½	cups

- Preheat oven to 180°C (350°F).
- Pour buttermilk over cereal and let stand until absorbed.
- In a medium bowl, mix flour, baking soda and salt; set aside.
- In a large bowl, combine oil, sugar, eggs and raisins. Add lentil purée, then the dry mixture and then the cereal mixture. Spoon into nonstick, medium-sized muffin tins, filling ¾ full.
- Bake 15-20 minutes.

20 servings

Yield:	20 muffins
Serving Size:	1 muffin
Preparation Time:	20 minutes
Pulse Product:	Laird Lentils

Nutritional Analysis (per serving)

Calories:	218	
Total Fat:	6.5	g
Saturated Fat:	1	g
Protein:	5.5	g
Carbohydrates:	37	g
Cholesterol:	27.5	mg
Sodium:	258.5	mg
Potassium:	154.5	mg
Folic Acid:	13	mcg
Total Fiber:	4	g
Soluble:	1.5	g
Insoluble:	2.5	g

Diabetic Food Choices

Starch:	1
1% Milk:	1
Sugar:	1½
Fats & Oils:	1

Lentil Rhubarb Strawberry Crisp, page 151

Lentil Apple Muffins

This recipe doubles very well.

1		**egg**	**1**	
125	**mL**	**canola oil**	**½**	**cup**
250	**mL**	**Laird Lentil purée**	**1**	**cup**
250	**mL**	**canned apple pie filling**	**1**	**cup**
175	**mL**	**whole-wheat flour**	**¾**	**cup**
175	**mL**	**all-purpose flour**	**¾**	**cup**
75	**mL**	**packed brown sugar**	**⅓**	**cup**
10	**mL**	**baking powder**	**2**	**tsp.**
5	**mL**	**baking soda**	**1**	**tsp.**
5	**mL**	**cinnamon**	**1**	**tsp.**
2	**mL**	**salt**	**½**	**tsp.**
1	**mL**	**ground allspice**	**¼**	**tsp.**
0.5	**mL**	**nutmeg**	**⅛**	**tsp.**

- Preheat oven to 200°C (400°F).
- Beat egg. Stir in oil. Add purée and apple filling.
- In a separate bowl, combine flours, sugar, baking powder, soda, cinnamon, salt, allspice and nutmeg.
- Stir dry mixture into purée mixture just until flour is moistened.
- Spray medium-sized muffin tins with non-stick vegetable spray. Spoon batter into muffin tins.
- Bake 15 minutes, or until top of muffin bounces back to the touch.

12 servings

Yield:	12 muffins
Serving Size:	1 muffin
Preparation Time:	20 minutes
Pulse Product:	Laird Lentils

Nutritional Analysis
(per serving)

Calories:	175	
Total Fat:	6	g
Saturated Fat:	1	g
Protein:	4.5	g
Carbohydrates:	28	g
Cholesterol:	46	mg
Sodium:	273.5	mg
Potassium:	127	mg
Folic Acid:	10.5	mcg
Total Fiber:	3	g
Soluble:	1	g
Insoluble:	2	g

Diabetic Food Choices

Starch:	1
Fruit & Vegetables:	1
Fats & Oils:	1

Cranberry Lentil Muffins

A Christmas specialty!

125	mL	cooked Laird Lentils	½ cup
50	mL	orange juice	¼ cup
500	mL	all-purpose flour	2 cups
15	mL	baking powder	1 tbsp.
2	mL	salt	½ tsp.
2	mL	cinnamon	½ tsp.
2	mL	ground allspice	½ tsp.
2	mL	pumpkin pie spice	½ tsp.
250	mL	cooked Laird Lentils	1 cup
50	mL	orange juice	¼ cup
125	mL	honey	½ cup
75	mL	canola oil	⅓ cup
2		eggs	2
398	mL	can whole cranberries, coarsely chopped	14 oz.

- Preheat oven to 200°C (400°F).
- In a blender, combine first quantities of lentils and orange juice. Purée until smooth.
- Sift together flour, baking powder, salt, cinnamon, allspice and pumpkin pie spice.
- In a separate bowl, mix together lentil purée, remaining lentils, orange juice, honey, oil, eggs and cranberries. Add to dry mixture, stirring only until dry ingredients are moistened. Spoon mixture into paper-lined medium-sized, muffin cups filling ¾ full.
- Bake 20-25 minutes, or until toothpick inserted in center comes out clean.

18 servings

Yield:	18 muffins
Serving Size:	1 muffin
Preparation Time:	20 minutes
Pulse Product:	Laird Lentils

Nutritional Analysis
(per serving)

Calories:	156	
Total Fat:	5	g
Saturated Fat:	0.5	g
Protein:	4	g
Carbohydrates:	26	g
Cholesterol:	30.5	g
Sodium:	153.5	mg
Potassium:	97	mg
Folic Acid:	10	mcg
Total Fiber:	2	g
Soluble:	0.5	g
Insoluble:	1.5	g

Diabetic Food Choices

Starch:	1½
Fats & Oils:	1

DESSERTS

Gluten-Free

Yield:	750 mL (3 cups)
Serving Size:	175 mL (¾ cup)
Preparation Time:	20 minutes
Pulse Product:	Green Split Peas

Nutritional Analysis
(per serving)

Calories:	346	
Total Fat:	25	g
Saturated Fat:	15	g
Protein:	7	g
Carbohydrates:	20	g
Cholesterol:	282.5	mg
Sodium:	142	mg
Potassium:	162	mg
Folic Acid:	20.5	mcg
Total Fiber:	2	g
Soluble:	0.5	g
Insoluble:	1.5	g

Diabetic Food Choices

Protein:	½
Starch:	1
Whole Milk:	½
Fats & Oils:	4

St. Patrick's Mousse

Would you believe it's delicious?

75	mL	granulated sugar	⅓	cup
25	mL	Grand Marnier liqueur	2	tbsp.
1	mL	unflavored gelatin powder	¼	tsp.
3		eggs, separated	3	
175	mL	Green Split Pea purée	¾	cup
500	mL	whipping cream	2	cups

- In a double boiler, combine sugar, liqueur, gelatin and egg yolks. Cook over medium heat until thick. Remove from heat, stir in purée and set aside.
- In a bowl, beat egg whites until stiff. Fold into pea mixture.
- Whip cream and fold into egg white mixture.
- Spoon mousse into parfait glasses. Refrigerate until set.
- Garnish with whipped cream before serving, if desired.

4 servings

Orange Lentil Chiffon

A *low-fat dessert.*

7	g	envelope unflavored gelatin (15 mL/1 tbsp.)	¼	oz.
50	mL	cold water	¼	cup
10.2	g	pkg. sugar-free orange jelly powder	⅓	oz.
250	mL	boiling water	1	cup
250	mL	Rose Lentil purée	1	cup
2		eggs, separated	2	
50	mL	granulated sugar	¼	cup
5	mL	pumpkin pie spice	1	tsp.
2	mL	cinnamon	¼	tsp.
300	mL	low-fat cottage cheese, puréed	1¼	cups
5	mL	granulated sugar	1	tsp.

Brown Sugar Frosting:

175	mL	low-fat cottage cheese, puréed	¾	cup
25	mL	low-fat yogurt	2	tbsp.
15	mL	brown sugar	1	tbsp.
		fruit for garnish		

- Dissolve gelatin in cold water.
- Add orange jelly powder and boiling water. Stir until dissolved. Set aside.
- In a medium saucepan, combine lentil purée, egg yolks, sugar and spices. Cook over low heat until thickened. Remove from heat.
- In a large bowl, combine cheese purée, lentil and gelatin mixtures. Cool to egg white consistency.
- In a bowl, beat egg whites until foamy. Add sugar and beat until soft peaks form. Fold into cooled mixture.
- Pour into 23 cm (9") pie plate. Chill.
- Combine all frosting ingredients. Spread over filling and garnish with mandarin orange sections, kiwi slices or blueberries. Cut into 8 wedges.
- **8 servings.**

Yield:	8 wedges
Serving Size:	1 wedge
Preparation Time:	45 minutes
Pulse Product:	Rose Lentils

Nutritional Analysis
(per serving)

Calories:	136	
Total Fat:	2	g
Saturated Fat:	1	g
Protein:	13	g
Carbohydrates:	17.5	g
Cholesterol:	71	mg
Sodium:	263	mg
Potassium:	156	mg
Folic Acid:	16	mcg
Total Fiber:	trace	
Soluble:	trace	
Insoluble:	trace	

Diabetic Food Choices

Protein:	1½
Starch:	1

146

Yield:	9 pieces
Serving Size:	1 piece
Preparation Time:	20 minutes
Pulse Product:	Laird Lentils

Nutritional Analysis
(per serving)

Calories:	330	
Total Fat:	17.5	g
Saturated Fat:	7	g
Protein:	6.5	g
Carbohydrates:	40.5	g
Cholesterol:	6	mg
Sodium:	177	mg
Potassium:	259	mg
Folic Acid:	11.5	mcg
Total Fiber:	2.5	g
Soluble:	0.5	g
Insoluble:	2	g

Diabetic Food Choices

Starch:	1
1% Milk:	1
Sugar:	2
Fats & Oils:	2½

Lentil Cloud

Float away on this heavenly dessert.

32		large marshmallows	32	
250	mL	Laird Lentil purée	1	cup
2	mL	pumpkin pie spice	½	tsp.
2	mL	cinnamon	½	tsp.
1	mL	ground ginger	¼	tsp.
0.5	mL	ground cloves	⅛	tsp.
250	mL	graham crumbs	1	cup
50	mL	melted margarine	¼	cup
125	mL	1% milk	½	cup
10	g	pkg. light dessert whip	⅓	oz.
125	mL	slivered almonds, toasted*	½	cup

- In a saucepan, combine marshmallows, lentil purée, pumpkin pie spice, cinnamon, ginger and cloves. Heat over low heat, stirring constantly, until mixture is smooth. Remove from heat and cool 15 minutes.
- In a bowl, combine graham crumbs and margarine. Press crumb mixture into a 20 cm (8") square cake pan.
- In another bowl, mix milk and dessert whip as per package instructions.
- Fold whipped topping into cooled lentil mixture. Spread over crumbs.
- Refrigerate 4 hours. Garnish with toasted almonds. Cut into 9 pieces.

9 servings

*To toast almonds, spread them on a nonstick cookie sheet and broil 3-4 minutes, stirring frequently.

Festive Cranberry Torte

A cool, light Christmas dessert.

Pecan Crumb Crust:

375	mL	graham crumbs	1½ cups
125	mL	chopped pecans	½ cup
50	mL	granulated sugar	¼ cup
90	mL	margarine, melted	6 tbsp.

Cranberry Bean Filling:

375	mL	cooked Great Northern Beans	1½ cups
125	mL	frozen cranberry cocktail concentrate	½ cup
50	mL	granulated sugar	¼ cup
5	mL	almond extract OR Grand Marnier	1 tsp.

Cranberry Cake:

375	mL	crushed fresh OR frozen cranberries	1½ cups
250	mL	granulated sugar	1 cup
2		egg whites	2
15	mL	frozen orange juice concentrate, thawed	1 tbsp.
5	mL	vanilla	1 tsp.
2	mL	salt	½ tsp.
250	mL	whipping cream	1 cup

Cranberry Glaze:

125	mL	cranberry cocktail concentrate	½ cup
125	mL	water	½ cup
15	mL	cornstarch	1 tbsp.

• Preheat oven to 180°C (350°F).

Filling Yield:	12 wedges
Serving Size:	1 wedge
Preparation Time:	45 minutes
Pulse Product:	Great Northern Beans

Nutritional Analysis (per serving)

Calories:	350	
Total Fat:	15	g
Saturated Fat:	4	g
Protein:	3	g
Carbohydrates:	55	g
Cholesterol:	13	mg
Sodium:	252.5	mg
Potassium:	148.5	mg
Folic Acid:	7	mcg
Total Fiber:	2.5	g
Soluble:	1	g
Insoluble:	1.5	g

Diabetic Food Choices

Starch:	1
Sugar:	4
Fats & Oils:	3

Festive Cranberry Torte

(Continued)

- To prepare crust, in a mixing bowl, combine graham crumbs, pecans, sugar and margarine. Press crust mixture onto the bottom and up the sides of a 20 cm (8") springform pan. Bake 10 minutes. Cool.
- To prepare bean layer, in a food processor, purée beans, cranberry cocktail, sugar and almond extract. Spread over cooled crust.
- To prepare cake, in a large mixing bowl combine cranberries and sugar; let stand 5 minutes. Add unbeaten egg whites, orange juice concentrate, vanilla and salt. Beat on low speed of electric mixer until frothy. Then beat at high speed 6-8 minutes, or until stiff peaks form (tips stand straight).
- In a small bowl, whip cream to soft peaks (tips curl over). Fold into the cranberry mixture. Turn into springform pan. Freeze firm.
- To prepare glaze, in a saucepan, combine cranberry cocktail, water and cornstarch. Bring to a boil, stir and cook until thick. Cool and drizzle over frozen dessert.
- Cut Torte into 12 wedges to serve.
12 servings

Lentil Cheesecake

Lentil purée is the "secret" ingredient.

Pecan Crumb Crust:

125	mL	graham crumbs	½ cup
75	mL	finely chopped pecans	⅓ cup
25	mL	margarine, melted	2 tbsp.
25	mL	brown sugar	2 tbsp.

Spiced Lentil Filling:

500	g	low-fat cream cheese	16 oz.
50	mL	brown sugar	¼ cup
50	mL	granulated sugar	¼ cup
2		eggs	2
250	mL	Laird Lentil purée	1 cup
5	mL	cinnamon	1 tsp.
1	mL	nutmeg	¼ tsp.
1	mL	pumpkin pie spice	¼ tsp.
15	mL	1% milk	1 tbsp.
7	mL	cornstarch	1½ tsp.

Orange Cream Cheese Icing:

250	g	spreadable low-fat cream cheese	8 oz.
25	mL	icing sugar	2 tbsp.
7	mL	orange liqueur	1½ tsp.
2	mL	grated orange rind	½ tsp.

- Combine crumbs, pecans, margarine and sugar. Press into and up sides of a 20 cm (8") springform pan. Chill.
- Preheat oven to 180°C (350°F).
- To prepare filling, with electric mixer, beat cream cheese and sugars until smooth. Beat in eggs, 1 at a time until just blended. Beat in remaining ingredients. Pour into pan.
- Bake 45 minutes, until center is just set.
- Remove cake from oven; run a knife around edge to loosen it from pan. Cool at room temperature.
- Beat all icing ingredients together. Spread over cooled cake. Cut into 12 wedges.

12 servings

Yield:	12 wedges
Serving Size:	1 wedge
Preparation Time:	30 minutes
Pulse Product:	Laird Lentils

Nutritional Analysis
(per serving)

Calories:	290	
Total Fat:	21	g
Saturated Fat:	10.5	g
Protein:	7	g
Carbohydrates:	21.5	g
Cholesterol:	94	mg
Sodium:	186	mg
Potassium:	168	mg
Folic Acid:	13	mcg
Total Fiber:	1.5	g
Soluble:	0.5	g
Insoluble:	1	g

Diabetic Food Choices

Protein:	½
Starch:	1
Sugar:	½
Fats & Oils:	3

Yield:	9 pieces
Serving Size:	1 piece
Preparation Time:	20 minutes
Pulse Product:	Rose Lentils

Nutritional Analysis
(per serving)

Calories:	342	
Total Fat:	12	g
Saturated Fat:	2	g
Protein:	7	g
Carbohydrates:	55.5	g
Cholesterol:	0	mg
Sodium:	150.5	mg
Potassium:	265.5	mg
Folic Acid:	21	mcg
Total Fiber:	2.5	g
Soluble:	1	g
Insoluble:	1.5	g

Diabetic Food Choices

Protein:	½
Starch:	2
Fruit & Vegetables:	1½
Sugar:	2
Fats & Oils:	2

Pictured on page 141.

Lentil Rhubarb Strawberry Crisp

If you are cleaning out the deep freeze, you can substitute any frozen fruit combination for rhubarb and strawberries.

250	mL	all-purpose flour	1 cup
250	mL	rolled oats (not instant)	1 cup
125	mL	brown sugar	½ cup
125	mL	margarine, melted	½ cup
5	mL	cinnamon	1 tsp.
500	mL	cooked Rose Lentils	2 cups
250	mL	diced frozen rhubarb	1 cup
250	mL	sliced frozen strawberries	1 cup
125	mL	granulated sugar	½ cup
25	mL	cornstarch	2 tbsp.
250	mL	water	1 cup
5	mL	vanilla	1 tsp.

- Preheat oven to 180°C (350°F).
- In a bowl, combine flour, oats, brown sugar, margarine and cinnamon. Mix thoroughly. Press half the mixture into a 20 cm (8" square) nonstick pan. Reserve remainder for topping.
- In a bowl, combine lentils, rhubarb and strawberries. Mix well. Spread over crumb base.
- In a medium saucepan, combine sugar and cornstarch. Stir in water. Cook over medium heat, stirring constantly until clear. Add vanilla. Pour over lentil mixture and top with remaining crumbs.
- Bake 60 minutes. Cool slightly and cut into 9 pieces.

9 servings

Lentil Custard Pie

Rhubarb spells spring!

50	mL	raisins	¼	cup
25	mL	orange juice	2	tbsp.
175	mL	granulated sugar	¾	cup
25	mL	melted margarine	2	tbsp.
2		eggs, lightly beaten	2	
375	mL	cooked Rose Lentils	1½	cups
375	mL	diced frozen rhubarb	1½	cups
50	mL	all-purpose flour	¼	cup
23	cm	uncooked pie shell	9"	

- Preheat oven to 180°C (350°F).
- In a small saucepan, combine raisins and orange juice. Cook over low heat until raisins plump up.
- In a bowl, cream sugar and margarine.
- Add eggs, lentils and rhubarb. Mix thoroughly. Add flour and raisin mixture. Mix.
- Turn filling into pie shell. Bake 50 minutes.
- Remove from heat and cool on wire rack. Cut into 8 wedges.

8 servings

Yield:	8 wedges
Serving Size:	1 wedge
Preparation Time:	15 minutes
Pulse Product:	Rose Lentils

Nutritional Analysis
(per serving)

Calories:	327	
Total Fat:	14	g
Saturated Fat:	4	g
Protein:	6.5	g
Carbohydrates:	47	g
Cholesterol:	71	mg
Sodium:	214.5	mg
Potassium:	201.5	mg
Folic Acid:	19.5	mcg
Total Fiber:	1.5	g
Soluble:	0.5	g
Insoluble:	1	g

Diabetic Food Choices

Protein:	½
Starch:	1
Fruit & Vegetables:	1
Sugar:	½
Fats & Oils:	2½

Yield:	8 wedges
Serving Size:	1 wedge
Preparation Time:	25 minutes
Pulse Product:	Rose Lentils

Nutritional Analysis
(per serving)

Calories:	294	
Total Fat:	13	g
Saturated Fat:	3	g
Protein:	6	g
Carbohydrates:	42	g
Cholesterol:	68	mg
Sodium:	234	mg
Potassium:	249	mg
Folic Acid:	21	mcg
Total Fiber:	5	g
Soluble:	1.5	g
Insoluble:	3.5	g

Diabetic Food Choices

Starch:	1
Fruit & Vegetables:	2½
Fats & Oils:	3

Lentil Kiwi Pie

This is a wonderful summertime dessert.

Crumb Crust:

250	mL	graham crumbs	1	cup
50	mL	margarine, melted	¼	cup
15	mL	granulated sugar	1	tbsp.

Lentil Filling:

50	mL	margarine	¼	cup
125	mL	granulated sugar	½	cup
2		egg yolks	2	
500	mL	Rose Lentil purée	2	cups
50	mL	cornstarch	¼	cup
50	mL	cold water	¼	cup
375	mL	boiling water	1½	cups
5	mL	vanilla	1	tsp.
175	mL	sliced kiwi	¾	cup
50	mL	sliced strawberries	¼	cup

- Preheat oven to 180°C (350°F).
- To prepare crust, combine graham crumbs, melted margarine and sugar. Press into a 23 cm (9") pie plate. Bake 7 minutes. Remove and cool.
- In a double boiler, melt margarine. Add sugar and egg yolks. Stir until thick. Add lentil purée, stirring until hot.
- Combine cornstarch and cold water to make a paste. Add to lentil mixture, stirring constantly until thick. Add boiling water, bring filling to a boil and boil 1 minute stirring constantly. Remove from heat. Stir in vanilla. Pour into pie shell.
- Cool and refrigerate.
- Just before serving garnish with kiwi and strawberries slices. Cut into 8 wedges.

8 servings

Piña Colada Cream Pie

Shake off the winter blues with this exotic dessert.

Honey Crumb Crust:

300	mL	graham crumbs	1¼	cups
50	mL	margarine, melted	¼	cup
25	mL	liquid honey	2	tbsp.

Piña Colada Filling:

625	mL	cooked Rose Lentils, drained	2½	cups
250	g	low-fat cream cheese	8	oz.
75	mL	liquid honey	⅓	cup
15	mL	canola oil	1	tbsp.
5	mL	cornstarch	1	tsp.
5	mL	vanilla	1	tsp.
2	mL	salt	½	tsp.
398	mL	can unsweetened crushed pineapple, drained	14	oz.
125	mL	shredded unsweetened coconut	½	cup

- Preheat oven to 180°C (350°F).
- To prepare crust, combine graham crumbs, margarine and honey. Mix well. Press into 23 cm (9") pie plate.
- In a food processor, combine lentils, cream cheese, honey, oil, cornstarch, vanilla and salt. Blend until puréed. Pour into mixing bowl. Stir in pineapple and coconut. Pour into pie shell.
- Bake 20 minutes.
- Remove from oven and cool. Cut into 6 wedges.

6 servings

Yield:	6 wedges
Serving Size:	1 wedge
Preparation Time:	25 minutes
Pulse Product:	Rose Lentils

Nutritional Analysis (per serving)

Calories:	515	
Total Fat:	28	g
Saturated Fat:	13	g
Protein:	12	g
Carbohydrates:	64	g
Cholesterol:	34	mg
Sodium:	484	mg
Potassium:	478.5	mg
Folic Acid:	33	mcg
Total Fiber:	4	g
Soluble:	1	g
Insoluble:	3	g

Diabetic Food Choices

Protein:	1
Starch:	2½
Sugar:	2
Fats & Oils:	5

Yield:	12 tarts	
Serving Size:	1 tart	
Preparation Time:	15 minutes	
Pulse Product:	Rose Lentils	

Nutritional Analysis
(per serving)

Calories:	177	
Total Fat:	10	g
Saturated Fat:	3.5	g
Protein:	4	g
Carbohydrates:	20	g
Cholesterol:	26	mg
Sodium:	181	mg
Potassium:	98.5	mg
Folic Acid:	9	mcg
Total Fiber:	2	g
Soluble:	0.5	g
Insoluble:	1.5	g

Diabetic Food Choices

Starch:	½
Fruit & Vegetables:	1
Fats & Oils:	2

Lentil Peach Tarts

For variety, dot each tart with 2 mL (½ tsp.) of unsweetened strawberry jam.

12	**frozen unbaked medium-sized tart shells**	**12**	
50	**mL**	**granulated sugar**	**¼ cup**
50	**mL**	**melted margarine**	**¼ cup**
5	**mL**	**lemon juice**	**1 tsp.**
1	**mL**	**salt**	**¼ tsp.**
1		**egg**	**1**
250	**mL**	**cooked Rose Lentils**	**1 cup**
175	**mL**	**cubed skinned peaches**	**¾ cup**
50	**mL**	**ground almonds**	**¼ cup**

- Preheat oven to 200°C (400°F).
- Place tart shells on cookie sheet and thaw 10 minutes. Bake tart shells 5 minutes. Remove from oven and let stand until filling is prepared.
- Reduce oven temperature to 180°C (350°F).
- In a bowl, cream sugar, margarine, lemon juice, salt and egg. Stir in lentils, peaches and almonds.
- Spoon filling into tart shells until full. Bake 30 minutes.
- Cool completely. Cover and refrigerate.
  12 servings

Lentil Sour Cream Pie

A variation of an old favorite.

Crumb Crust:

300	mL	graham crumbs	1¼ cups
50	mL	margarine, melted	¼ cup
5	mL	granulated sugar	1 tsp.

Raisin Sour Cream Filling:

175	mL	granulated sugar	¾ cup
15	mL	all-purpose flour	1 tbsp.
10	mL	pumpkin pie spice	2 tsp.
5	mL	cinnamon	1 tsp.
2	mL	nutmeg	½ tsp.
2	mL	ground allspice	½ tsp.
1	mL	salt	¼ tsp.
2		eggs, slightly beaten	2
375	mL	Laird Lentil purée	1½ cups
175	mL	low-fat sour cream	¾ cup
175	mL	raisins	¾ cup

- Preheat oven to 200°C (400°F).
- To prepare crust, in a bowl, combine crumbs, margarine and sugar. Mix. Press into 22 cm (9 inch) pie plate. Chill 10 minutes in refrigerator.
- To prepare filling, in a bowl, combine sugar, flour, pumpkin pie spice, cinnamon, nutmeg, allspice and salt.
- In a separate bowl, mix together eggs, lentil purée, sour cream and raisins. Stir in sugar mixture. Pour into crust.
- Bake 50 minutes, or until knife inserted in middle of pie comes out clean.
- Remove and cool. Refrigerate. Slice into 8 wedges.

8 servings

Yield:	8 wedges
Serving Size:	1 wedge
Preparation Time:	20 minutes
Pulse Product:	Laird Lentils

Nutritional Analysis
(per serving)

Calories:	324	
Total Fat:	11	g
Saturated Fat:	3.5	g
Protein:	6	g
Carbohydrates:	55	g
Cholesterol:	44	mg
Sodium:	236	mg
Potassium:	312	mg
Folic Acid:	16	mcg
Total Fiber:	4	g
Soluble:	1	g
Insoluble:	3	g

Diabetic Food Choices

Protein:	½
Starch:	1½
Sugar:	3
Fats & Oils:	2

Yield:	12 wedges
Serving Size:	1 wedge
Preparation Time:	20 minutes
Pulse Product:	Laird Lentils

Nutritional Analysis
(per serving)

Calories:	215	
Total Fat:	9.5	g
Saturated Fat:	2	g
Protein:	4.5	g
Carbohydrates:	31	g
Cholesterol:	68.5	mg
Sodium:	160	mg
Potassium:	133.5	mg
Folic Acid:	13	mcg
Total Fiber:	2.5	g
Soluble:	0.5	g
Insoluble:	2	g

Diabetic Food Choices

Starch:	2
Fats & Oils:	2

Lentil Fudge Pie

This is soooo good!

Crumb Crust:

175	mL	graham crumbs	¾	cup
45	mL	melted margarine	3	tbsp.
10	mL	granulated sugar	2	tsp.

Fudge Filling:

50	mL	cocoa	¼	cup
50	mL	melted margarine	¼	cup
125	mL	granulated sugar	½	cup
125	mL	corn syrup	½	cup
5	mL	vanilla	1	tsp.
3		eggs, separated	3	
375	mL	Laird Lentil purée	1½	cups

- Preheat oven to 180°C (350°F).
- In a bowl, combine crumbs, margarine and sugar. Press into 23 cm (9") pie plate. Chill.
- In a bowl, combine cocoa and margarine. Mix well. Add sugar, syrup, vanilla and egg yolks. Beat together with electric mixer for 2 minutes on medium speed. Fold in lentil purée.
- In another bowl, beat egg whites until stiff. Fold into lentil purée mixture. Turn into pie shell.
- Bake 40 minutes, or until knife inserted comes out clean.
- Remove and cool thoroughly. Refrigerate.
- Use a wet knife to slice pie into 12 wedges.
12 servings

Lentil Cake Roll

A quick and easy cake roll!

175	mL	all-purpose flour	¾ cup
5	mL	baking powder	1 tsp.
2	mL	cinnamon	½ tsp.
2	mL	pumpkin pie spice	½ tsp.
2	mL	nutmeg	½ tsp.
2	mL	ground ginger	½ tsp.
1	mL	salt	¼ tsp.
3		eggs	3
175	mL	granulated sugar	¾ cup
150	mL	Laird Lentil purée	⅔ cup
7	mL	lemon juice	1½ tsp.
125	mL	chopped walnuts	½ cup
125	mL	low-fat cream cheese, at room temperature	½ cup
125	mL	unsweetened orange marmalade	½ cup
50	mL	icing sugar	¼ cup

- Preheat oven to 190°C (375°F).
- In a bowl, combine flour, baking powder, spices and salt. Set aside.
- With electric mixer beat eggs 5 minutes. Gradually add sugar and continue beating. Stir in purée and lemon juice.
- Fold in dry ingredients.
- Spray a 40 x 25 cm (10½ x 15½") jelly roll pan with nonstick spray and flour it. Pour batter into pan. Sprinkle walnuts over batter; bake 15 minutes, until cake springs back to the touch.
- Sprinkle tea towel with icing sugar. Turn cake out onto towel, nut side down. Roll cake in towel. Allow to cool.
- In a bowl, cream together cream cheese, marmalade and icing sugar. Add a little milk if necessary to achieve a spreadable mixture.
- Unroll cake and spread with cheese mixture.
- Reroll cake and cut into 14 slices.

14 servings

Yield:	14 slices
Serving Size:	1 slice
Preparation Time:	20 minutes
Pulse Product:	Laird Lentils

Nutritional Analysis (per serving)

Calories:	170	
Total Fat:	6	g
Saturated Fat:	2	g
Protein:	4	g
Carbohydrates:	27	g
Cholesterol:	64	mg
Sodium:	98	mg
Potassium:	85.5	mg
Folic Acid:	9.5	mcg
Total Fiber:	1	g
Soluble:	0.5	g
Insoluble:	0.5	g

Diabetic Food Choices

Starch:	1
Sugar:	1
Fats & Oils:	1

Yield:	24 pieces
Serving Size:	1 piece
Preparation Time:	20 minutes
Pulse Product:	Rose Lentils

Nutritional Analysis
(per serving)

Calories:	149	
Total Fat:	9	g
Saturated Fat:	1	g
Protein:	3	g
Carbohydrates:	17	g
Cholesterol:	0	mg
Sodium:	131	mg
Potassium:	150	mg
Folic Acid:	8	mcg
Total Fiber:	1.5	g
Soluble:	0.5	g
Insoluble:	1	g

Diabetic Food Choices

Starch:	1
Sugar:	1
Fats & Oils:	1½

Spicy Lentil Cake

A spicy, nutritious cake which is a flavorful addition to any lunch box.

375	mL	Rose Lentil purée	1½ cups
175	mL	canola oil	¾ cup
125	mL	mashed banana	½ cup
125	mL	packed brown sugar	½ cup
500	mL	whole-wheat flour	2 cups
10	mL	baking powder	2 tsp.
5	mL	baking soda	1 tsp.
5	mL	ground allspice	1 tsp.
2	mL	salt	½ tsp.
125	mL	chopped walnuts	½ cup
250	mL	finely grated carrot	1 cup

- Preheat oven to 180°C (350°F).
- In a mixing bowl, combine lentil purée, oil, banana and brown sugar until well blended.
- In a separate bowl, combine flour, baking powder, soda, allspice and salt. Mix thoroughly. Beat into lentil mixture a little at a time. Stir in walnuts. Stir in carrot.
- Turn into a 22 x 34 cm (9 x 13") nonstick baking dish.
- Bake 30 minutes, or until toothpick inserted in center comes out clean.

24 servings

Banana Bean Cake

No flour, but it works!

75	mL	canola oil	⅓	cup
150	mL	granulated sugar	⅔	cup
1		banana, mashed	1	
2		eggs	2	
500	mL	Great Northern Bean purée	2	cups
5	mL	vanilla	1	tsp.
2	mL	salt	½	tsp.
375	mL	quick-cooking oats	1½	cups
5	mL	baking soda	1	tsp.
75	mL	chocolate chips	⅓	cup

- Preheat oven to 180°C (350°F).
- In a bowl, beat together oil and sugar until light and fluffy. Blend in banana, eggs, purée and vanilla.
- In a separate bowl, combine salt, oats and soda. Gradually add to the bean purée mixture, mixing well.
- Stir in chocolate chips. Pour into a 22 x 34 cm (9 x 13") nonstick cake pan.
- Bake 25 minutes.
- Let cool completely before cutting into 24 squares.
  24 servings.

Yield:	24 pieces
Serving Size:	1 piece
Preparation Time:	20 minutes
Pulse Product:	Great Northern Beans

Nutritional Analysis
(per serving)

Calories:	103	
Total Fat:	4	g
Saturated Fat:	trace	
Protein:	2	g
Carbohydrates:	15	g
Cholesterol:	23	mg
Sodium:	96	mg
Potassium:	95	mg
Folic Acid:	7	mcg
Total Fiber:	2	g
Soluble:	1	g
Insoluble:	1	g

Diabetic Food Choices

Starch:	1
Fats & Oils:	1

Yield:	15 pieces
Serving Size:	1 piece
Preparation Time:	25 minutes
Pulse Product:	Pink Beans

Nutritional Analysis
(per serving)

Calories:	428	
Total Fat:	26	g
Saturated Fat:	5	g
Protein:	4.5	g
Carbohydrates:	47	g
Cholesterol:	73	mg
Sodium:	250	mg
Potassium:	225	mg
Folic Acid:	12	mcg
Total Fiber	3	g
Soluble:	1	g
Insoluble:	2	g

Diabetic Food Choices

Starch:	1
Fruit & Vegetables:	2
Sugar:	1
Fats & Oils:	5

Apple Bean Cake

A lovely moist cake.

375 mL	cooked Pink Beans	1½ cups
75 mL	apple juice	⅓ cup
175 mL	canola oil	¾ cup
175 mL	granulated sugar	¾ cup
175 mL	brown sugar	¾ cup
2	eggs	2
5 mL	vanilla	1 tsp.
250 mL	whole-wheat flour	1 cup
125 mL	all-purpose flour	½ cup
10 mL	baking powder	2 tsp.
5 mL	cinnamon	1 tsp.
2 mL	salt	½ tsp.
2 mL	ground cloves	½ tsp.
500 mL	peeled, grated apple	2 cups

Coconut Pecan Topping:

125 mL	brown sugar	½ cup
150 mL	margarine	⅔ cup
2	egg yolks	2
125 mL	shredded coconut	½ cup
125 mL	pecans	½ cup

- Preheat oven to 180°C (350°F).
- Purée beans and apple juice until smooth.
- In a large mixing bowl, combine oil, sugars and eggs. Beat until well blended. Add bean purée and vanilla.
- In a separate bowl, combine flours, baking powder, cinnamon, salt and cloves. Add to bean mixture. Mix well. Stir in apple.
- Pour into a greased 18 x 28 cm (7 x 11") baking pan. Bake 50-60 minutes.
- To prepare topping, in a saucepan over medium heat combine sugar, margarine and egg yolks. Cook until thick. Stir in coconut and nuts. Spread over cooled cake. Cut into 15 pieces.

15 servings

Lentil Applesauce Squares

A great way to use up leftover lentil purée and applesauce.

175	mL	brown sugar	½	cup
125	mL	canola oil	½	cup
2		eggs	2	
250	mL	Eston Lentil purée	1	cup
125	mL	applesauce	½	cup
500	mL	all-purpose flour	2	cups
125	mL	raisins	½	cup
250	mL	chopped apple	1	cup
50	mL	chopped walnuts	¼	cup
5	mL	baking powder	1	tsp.
5	mL	cinnamon	1	tsp.
5	mL	pumpkin pie spice	1	tsp.
2	mL	nutmeg	½	tsp.
2	mL	baking soda	½	tsp.
2	mL	salt	½	tsp.
9		walnut halves	9	

- Preheat oven to 180°C (350°F).
- In a mixing bowl, cream together sugar and oil. Stir in eggs then lentils and applesauce.
- Blend in flour, raisins, apple, walnuts, baking powder, cinnamon, pumpkin pie spice, nutmeg, soda and salt. Spread mixture into 20 cm (8") square baking dish which has been sprayed with nonstick vegetable spray. Garnish with walnut halves.
- Bake 45 minutes, or until firm to touch. Remove and cool. Cut into 9 squares.

9 servings

Yield:	9 squares
Serving Size:	1 square
Preparation Time:	20 minutes
Pulse Product:	Eston Lentils

Nutritional Analysis
(per serving)

Calories:	396	
Total Fat:	17	g
Saturated Fat:	2	g
Protein:	7.5	g
Carbohydrates:	56.5	g
Cholesterol:	61	mg
Sodium:	215	mg
Potassium:	278	mg
Folic Acid:	16	mcg
Total Fiber:	5	g
Soluble:	2	g
Insoluble:	3	g

Diabetic Food Choices

Protein:	½
Starch:	2
Sugar:	2
Fats & Oils:	3

Lentil Raspberry Bars

Versatile — use macadamias or pecans.

Base:

325	mL	all-purpose flour	1⅓	cups
50	mL	granulated sugar	¼	cup
2	mL	baking powder	½	tsp.
1	mL	salt	¼	tsp.
125	mL	margarine	½	cup
1		egg, slightly beaten	1	
125	mL	low-sugar raspberry jam	½	cup

Lentil Filling:

250	mL	Laird Lentil purée	1	cup
250	mL	brown sugar	1	cup
50	mL	all-purpose flour	¼	cup
7	mL	baking powder	1½	tsp.
2	mL	vanilla	½	tsp.
1	mL	salt	¼	tsp.
2		eggs, beaten	2	
125	mL	shredded coconut	½	cup
125	mL	chopped macadamia nuts OR pecans	½	cup

- Preheat oven to 190°C (375°F).
- Combine flour, sugar, baking powder and salt. Cut margarine into flour mixture until coarse crumbs form. Stir in egg. Mix thoroughly with hands.
- Press base evenly into 22 x 34 cm (9 x 13") baking dish. Bake 10 minutes.
- Remove; cool slightly. Spread jam over base.
- Reduce oven to 180°C (350°F).
- Combine lentil purée, sugar, flour, baking powder, vanilla, salt and eggs. Mix well. Mix in coconut and nuts. Spread carefully over raspberry jam.
- Bake 25 minutes, or until firm.
- Remove and cool before cutting. Cut into 18 bars.

18 servings

Great Northern Chocolate Squares

For chocolate lovers!

Shortbread Crust:

75	mL	margarine	⅓ cup
250	mL	all-purpose flour	1 cup
15	mL	granulated sugar	1 tbsp.

Chocolate Topping:

50	mL	margarine	¼ cup
250	mL	granulated sugar	1 cup
2		eggs	2
15	mL	corn syrup	1 tbsp.
250	mL	Great Northern Bean purée	1 cup
45	mL	cocoa powder	3 tbsp.
1	mL	salt	¼ tsp.
5	mL	vanilla	1 tsp.
50	mL	walnut pieces	¼ cup

- Preheat oven to 180°C (350°F).
- To prepare crust: In a bowl, cut margarine into flour and sugar until crumbly. Press into a 18 x 28 cm (7 x 11") nonstick cake pan.
- Bake 15 minutes. Set aside to cool.
- To prepare topping: In a bowl, cream margarine with sugar. Add eggs and syrup and beat 1½ minutes with electric mixer.
- On low speed, blend in bean purée, cocoa powder, salt and vanilla.
- Pour onto crust, sprinkle with walnut pieces.
- Bake 30 minutes, or until firm.
- Cool. Cut into 35 squares.

35 servings

Yield:	35 squares
Serving Size:	1 square
Preparation Time:	25 minutes
Pulse Product:	Great Northern Beans

Nutritional Analysis (per serving)

Calories:	89	
Total Fat:	4	g
Saturated Fat:	1	g
Protein:	1	g
Carbohydrates:	12	g
Cholesterol:	15.5	mg
Sodium:	60	mg
Potassium:	32	mg
Folic Acid:	3	mcg
Total Fiber:	0.5	g
Soluble:	trace	
Insoluble:	trace	

Diabetic Food Choices

Starch:	½
Sugar:	½
Fats & Oils:	1

Lentil Granola Bars

Great for kids' lunches!

150	**mL**	**shredded coconut**	**⅔**	**cup**
250	**mL**	**chopped walnuts**	**1**	**cup**
500	**mL**	**quick-cooking rolled oats**	**2**	**cups**
250	**mL**	**brown sugar**	**1**	**cup**
75	**mL**	**all-bran cereal**	**⅓**	**cup**
175	**mL**	**Laird Lentil purée**	**¾**	**cup**
125	**mL**	**canola oil**	**½**	**cup**
1		**egg, slightly beaten**	**1**	

- Place rack in center of oven. Preheat oven to 180°C (350°F).
- In a mixing bowl, combine coconut, walnuts, oats, brown sugar and cereal.
- Add lentil purée, oil and egg. Mix just until dry ingredients are moistened.
- Spread over a 25 x 40 cm (10½ x 15½") nonstick cookie sheet. Bake 30 minutes, or until lightly browned.
- Cut, while still warm, into 35 bars.
  35 servings

Yield: 35 bars

Serving Size: 1 bar

Preparation Time: 25 minutes

Pulse Product: Laird Lentils

Nutritional Analysis
(per serving)

Calories:	108	
Total Fat:	7	g
Saturated Fat:	1.5	g
Protein:	2	g
Carbohydrates:	11	g
Cholesterol:	8	mg
Sodium:	9	mg
Potassium:	77	mg
Folic Acid:	4	mcg
Total Fiber:	0.5	g
Soluble:	trace	
Insoluble:	0.5	g

Diabetic Food Choices

Starch:	1
Fats & Oils:	1

Lentil Oatmeal Chocolate Chippers

*A high-fiber chocolate chip cookie
kids will love.*

250	mL	brown sugar	1	cup
175	mL	margarine	¾	cup
1		egg	1	
7	mL	vanilla	1½	tsp.
175	mL	Eston Lentil purée	¾	cup
375	mL	all-purpose flour	1½	cups
2	mL	salt	½	tsp.
5	mL	baking soda	1	tsp.
500	mL	quick-cooking rolled oats	2	cups
375	mL	chocolate chips	1½	cups
175	mL	chopped pecans	¾	cup

- Preheat oven to 190°C (375°F).
- In a bowl, cream together sugar and margarine. Add egg and mix just until blended. Add vanilla and lentil purée, and mix until blended.
- Sift flour, salt and soda together.
- Add flour mixture ⅓ at a time to creamed mixture. Mix on low until just blended.
- Add oats, chocolate chips and pecans, and blend lightly.
- Scoop 5 mL (1 tsp.) portions of dough onto a greased cookie sheet, 2.5 cm (1") apart, and flatten with a fork.
- Bake 12-15 minutes. Do not overbake.

36 servings

Yield:	36 cookies
Serving Size:	1 cookie
Preparation Time:	30 minutes
Pulse Product:	Eston Lentils

Nutritional Analysis (per serving)

Calories:	154	
Total Fat:	8.5	g
Saturated Fat:	1	g
Protein:	2.5	g
Carbohydrates:	18	g
Cholesterol:	7.5	mg
Sodium:	128	mg
Potassium:	99	mg
Folic Acid:	4.5	mcg
Total Fiber:	0.5	g
Soluble:	trace	
Insoluble:	0.5	g

Diabetic Food Choices

| Starch: | 1 |
| Fats & Oils: | 1½ |

Yield:	60 cookies
Serving Size:	1 cookie
Preparation Time:	20 minutes
Pulse Product:	Navy Beans

Nutritional Analysis
(per serving)

Calories:	86	
Total Fat:	4	g
Saturated Fat:	1	g
Protein:	1	g
Carbohydrates:	11	g
Cholesterol:	9	mg
Sodium:	86	mg
Potassium:	73	mg
Folic Acid:	4	mcg
Total Fiber:	0.5	g
Soluble:	trace	
Insoluble:	trace	

Diabetic Food Choices

Starch:	½
Sugar:	1
Fats & Oils:	½

Oatmeal Bean Chip Cookies

These cookies freeze well.

375	mL	all-purpose flour	1½	cups
250	mL	quick-cooking oats	1	cup
5	mL	baking soda	1	tsp.
2	mL	salt	½	tsp.
2	mL	cinnamon	½	tsp.
250	mL	chocolate chips	1	cup
125	mL	raisins	½	cup
250	mL	margarine	1	cup
250	mL	brown sugar	1	cup
2		eggs	2	
5	mL	vanilla	1	tsp.
227	mL	can Baked Beans in molasses, mashed	8	oz.

- Preheat oven to 180°C (350°F).
- In a bowl, combine flour, oats, soda, salt, cinnamon, chocolate chips and raisins. Mix well and set aside.
- Cream margarine. Add brown sugar and mix well. Add eggs and vanilla and continue mixing.
- Stir in beans thoroughly.
- Add half the dry ingredients and mix with a spoon until well blended. Add remaining dry ingredients and continue mixing.
- Drop 10 mL (2 tsp.) portions of batter onto a nonstick cookie sheet.
- Bake 14-16 minutes, or until lightly browned.
60 servings

Lentil Raisin Drops

Store in an airtight container to prevent cookies from drying out.

250	mL	raisins	1	cup
125	mL	orange juice	½	cup
2	mL	baking soda	½	tsp.
175	mL	brown sugar	¾	cup
125	mL	margarine	½	cup
1		egg	1	
5	mL	vanilla	1	tsp.
375	mL	all-purpose flour	1½	cups
2	mL	baking powder	½	tsp.
2	mL	cinnamon	½	tsp.
1	mL	salt	¼	tsp.
0.5	mL	nutmeg	⅛	tsp.
175	mL	Eston Lentil purée	¾	cup
125	mL	chopped walnuts	½	cup

- Preheat oven to 180°C (350°F).
- In a saucepan, combine raisins and orange juice. Bring to a gentle boil. Cook, uncovered, 5 minutes. Remove from heat and stir in soda. Cool.
- In a large mixing bowl, cream together sugar and margarine. Beat in egg and vanilla.
- In a separate bowl, combine flour, baking powder, cinnamon, salt and nutmeg. Stir into sugar mixture. Mix in lentil purée, walnuts and raisins.
- Drop batter by 15 mL (1 tbsp.) portions on an ungreased cookie sheet about 3 cm (1¼") apart.
- Bake 10-15 minutes, or until lightly browned on the bottom.

40 servings

Yield:	40 cookies
Serving Size:	1 cookie
Preparation Time:	20 minutes
Pulse Product:	Eston Lentils

Nutritional Analysis
(per serving)

Calories:	84	
Total Fat:	3.5	g
Saturated Fat:	0.5	g
Protein:	1.5	g
Carbohydrates:	12.5	g
Cholesterol:	7	mg
Sodium:	57	mg
Potassium:	75.5	mg
Folic Acid:	4	mcg
Total Fiber:	1	g
Soluble:	0.5	g
Insoluble:	0.5	g

Diabetic Food Choices

Starch:	1
Fats & Oils:	½

Yield:	48 cookies
Serving Size:	2 cookies
Preparation Time:	20 minutes
Pulse Product:	Kidney Beans

Nutritional Analysis
(per serving)

Calories:	85	
Total Fat:	4	g
Saturated Fat:	0.5	g
Protein:	1	g
Carbohydrates:	12	g
Cholesterol:	0	mg
Sodium:	63	mg
Potassium:	56	mg
Folic Acid:	2.5	mcg
Total Fiber:	0.5	g
Soluble:	trace	
Insoluble:	trace	

Diabetic Food Choices

Starch:	½
Sugar:	½
Fats & Oils:	½

High Five Cookies

For variety, make a depression in the centre of the cookie with your thumb and fill with raspberry jam.

125	mL	margarine	½	cup
250	mL	granulated sugar	1	cup
2	mL	vanilla	1	tsp.
398	mL	can Kidney Beans, rinsed and drained	14	oz.
250	mL	quick-cooking rolled oats	1	cup
250	mL	all-purpose flour	1	cup
15	mL	baking powder	1	tbsp.
2	mL	salt	½	tsp.
250	mL	raisins	1	cup
250	mL	chopped walnuts	1	cup

- Preheat oven to 180°C (350°F).
- In a bowl, cream margarine, sugar and vanilla.
- Mash beans in a bowl. Mix in oats, flour, baking powder, salt, raisins and walnuts.
- Add bean mixture to margarine mixture. Mix well.
- Drop by 15 mL (1 tbsp.) portions onto a non-stick cookie sheet. Bake 20 minutes.

48 servings

Index

***All Gluten-Free recipes are identified with an
asterisk.**

A Great Gift Idea

DISCOVER THE PULSE POTENTIAL _______________________ x $12.95 = $__________

THE AMAZING LEGUME _____________________________ x $11.95 = $__________

Postage and handling____(total order)_________________________________ = $______3.00__

Subtotal ____ = $__________

In Canada add 7% GST ____________________________(Subtotal x .07) = $__________

Total enclosed ____ = $__________

U.S. and international orders payable in U.S. funds./ Price is subject to change.

NAME: ____

STREET: ____

CITY: ___________________________ PROV./STATE _________________________

COUNTRY ___________________________ POSTAL CODE/ZIP _________________________

Please make cheque or money order payable to: **The Saskatchewan Pulse Crop Development Board**
P.O. Box 516
Regina, Saskatchewan
Canada S4P 3A2

For fund raising or volume rate purchases, contact
THE SASKATCHEWAN PULSE CROP DEVELOPMENT BOARD
Please allow 2-3 weeks for delivery.

A Great Gift Idea

DISCOVER THE PULSE POTENTIAL _______________________ x $12.95 = $__________

THE AMAZING LEGUME _____________________________ x $11.95 = $__________

Postage and handling____(total order)_________________________________ = $______3.00__

Subtotal ____ = $__________

In Canada add 7% GST ____________________________(Subtotal x .07) = $__________

Total enclosed ____ = $__________

U.S. and international orders payable in U.S. funds./ Price is subject to change.

NAME: ____

STREET: ____

CITY: ___________________________ PROV./STATE _________________________

COUNTRY ___________________________ POSTAL CODE/ZIP _________________________

Please make cheque or money order payable to: **The Saskatchewan Pulse Crop Development Board**
P.O. Box 516
Regina, Saskatchewan
Canada S4P 3A2

For fund raising or volume rate purchases, contact
THE SASKATCHEWAN PULSE CROP DEVELOPMENT BOARD
Please allow 2-3 weeks for delivery.

THE AMAZING LEGUME

COOKING WITH LENTILS, DRY BEANS & DRY PEAS

**By Alice Jenner,
B. Sc. (H.E.), P.Dt. Dip. in Nut.**

Long treasured for their low-calorie, cholesterol-free, high-fiber, iron, vitamin and protein content, flavorful legume dishes are now sought after by gourmet cooks. This inspiring collection of delicious recipes uses lentils in appetizers, soups, salads, entrées, side dishes and even desserts. They range from simple and practical to elegant and extraordinary. Health-conscious consumers are now using legumes in weight-watchers, heart disease, diabetes and low-salt diets.

Retail Price: $11.95   6" x 9"
136 pages   5 colored photographs

THE AMAZING LEGUME

COOKING WITH LENTILS, DRY BEANS & DRY PEAS

**By Alice Jenner,
B. Sc. (H.E.), P.Dt. Dip. in Nut.**

Long treasured for their low-calorie, cholesterol-free, high-fiber, iron, vitamin and protein content, flavorful legume dishes are now sought after by gourmet cooks. This inspiring collection of delicious recipes uses lentils in appetizers, soups, salads, entrées, side dishes and even desserts. They range from simple and practical to elegant and extraordinary. Health-conscious consumers are now using legumes in weight-watchers, heart disease, diabetes and low-salt diets.

Retail Price: $11.95   6" x 9"
136 pages   5 colored photographs